HEART
WHISPERS

HEART
WHISPERS

BENEDICTINE
WISDOM
FOR TODAY

ELIZABETH J. CANHAM

UPPER
ROOM BOOKS™
NASHVILLE

HEART WHISPERS
Benedictine Wisdom for Today
Copyright © 1999 by Elizabeth J. Canham
All rights reserved.

The Upper Room® Website http://www.upperroom.org

UPPER ROOM®, UPPER ROOM BOOKS™ and design logos are trademarks owned by the Upper Room®, Nashville, Tennessee. All rights reserved.

Scripture quotations not otherwise identified are from the New Revised Standard Version of the Bible, copyright © 1989 by the Division of Christian Education, National Council of the Churches of Christ in the United States of America. Used by permission.

All scripture quotations designated BCP are taken from *The Book of Common Prayer* (Episcopal), published by The Church Hymnal Corporation, New York, 1979.

All scripture quotations designated AP are the author's paraphrase.

"Psalm of the Salt Marsh" from *Limulus* by Maxwell Corydon Wheat Jr. Used by permission of the author.

Cover design: Gore Studio, Inc.
Cover transparency: © Mark Lewis / Picturesque
Second printing: 2000

LIBRARY OF CONGRESS CATALOGING-IN-PUBLICATION DATA

Canham, Elizabeth, 1939–
   Heart whispers : benedictine wisdom for today / Elizabeth Canham.
      p.   cm.
   Includes bibliographical references.
   ISBN 0-8358-0892-0
   1. Benedict, Saint, Abbot of Monte Cassino. Regula. I. Title.
BX3004.Z5C335 1999   99-21609
255'.106—DC21   CIP

Printed in the United States of America

I dedicate this book to all heart listeners who have joined me at Stillpoint for Benedictine gatherings. I am grateful for their faithful Christian discipleship in ordinary places through application of the Rule to contemporary life.

CONTENTS

PREFACE

LEARNING TO LISTEN with the heart moves us from the role of observers and enables us to become participants with the Creator in a world full of grace and possibility. I am grateful to all those who have opened up for me this vision of hope-filled journeying. From my no-nonsense grandmother I learned the importance of truth and integrity and from her daughter, my mother, a passion for the earth and all creatures that speak so eloquently of God's love. Fifteen years spent in a biblically centered church gave me a lasting love for the scriptures, and several wise spiritual guides supported my journey beyond fundamentalism and nurtured my relationship with Christ the Word who speaks freedom. Five years of living as a monastic oblate in a Benedictine community offered a formation experience that wove many strands of my faith journey together, and I owe my thanks to the Order of the Holy Cross for offering that opportunity and for introducing me to Saint Benedict.

Heart Whispers came into being after a conversation with John Mogabgab, editor of *Weavings* journal, who suggested that articles I had written over the years might become part of a larger publication on Benedictine spirituality. I am grateful to John for encouraging my writing and for connecting me with staff at The Upper Room®. Those who have attended the five diocesan Benedictine Experiences and numerous Benedictine Days we have offered in western North Carolina have also contributed to this book as they shared personal experiences of interpreting the Rule of Saint Benedict in diverse life situations. Finally I want to thank Mary Baumeister for her patient work on the manuscript and the Board of Directors at Stillpoint Ministries who have added their encouragement along the way. To all of us Saint Benedict says, "Prefer nothing whatever to Christ," and the purpose of this book is to encourage each of us daily to choose the Christ-path as we "hasten towards our heavenly home."

INTRODUCTION

Saint Benedict
A Man for All Seasons

How much is enough? In a culture that encourages acquisitiveness through an advertising industry that tells us we need more, better, and faster products, how can Christian believers make choices free from the compulsion to stockpile things? When obsession with food, diets, and exercise leads to overindulgence or abuse of our bodies, what wisdom will enable us to cherish our physical being as a gift from God? As competition drives us in the sports arena, corporate world, job market, or beauty pageant, how can we recapture a sense of community and mutual respect? If we always rush, achieve, grasp, or fill the hours with mindless busy-ness, how shall we hear the still small voice of our loving Creator who is always inviting us to fullness of life? Saint Benedict's words offer us a remedy for the sickness of soul that results from life lived out of kilter with the natural rhythms of our deepest being. He calls us to embody balance, to bring our being and our doing into harmony as we learn to hear God speak not only through intentional times of stillness but also in the humdrum, ordinary events of our days.

Balance, or resonance, characterizes the Rule that Benedict wrote to guide his community living in northern Italy during the mid-sixth century C.E. Unlike some of the extreme ascetics of the desert, Benedict calls for moderation in all things and says that in drawing up the Rule he intends "nothing harsh, nothing burdensome."[1] He deals with so many issues that touch our lives today: attitudes toward work, the need for recreation, appropriate quantities of food and drink, adequate rest, respect for one another, time for silence, the place of study in order to grow as faithful Christians, and a willingness to listen attentively to other members of the community so that shared wisdom and gifts enrich all. Above all, Benedict clearly believes that God is both the center and the circumference of life together, intimately present yet also beyond and always inviting us to stretch and grow more fully into Christ.

This book will explore some major themes in the Rule of Saint Benedict, allowing them to address us as we also attempt to follow the Christian way. Most of us are not called to the cloister, yet we find the practical common sense of Saint Benedict and his commitment to finding the holy in the ordinary readily accessible to us. Even the three monastic vows, stability, conversion of life, obedience, translate readily to life in the world. All of us need an anchor, a place of inner security in the midst of a mobile, transitory world, but as we consent to stability, to being where we are instead of escaping to some temporary bolt-hole, we are called to conversion.

We may need to change our inclination toward escape, our desire to avoid confrontation, or our readiness to compromise our discipleship. And certainly obedience to the word of God is a promise we need to make again and again as we get pulled aside by the insidious voices that suggest God's way means deprivation instead of gift. The Rule of Saint Benedict embodies the conviction that we have all we need—we have enough. Conversely Benedict also tells us that we need all we have, for all our gifts, personal history, and life experience make up the raw material out of which we are formed in God's image and grow together in community.

Learning to Let Go

Knowing that we have enough takes us out of the never-ending tension created by greed, out of the constant envy of others that causes us to overlook our own riches, and out of the turmoil of unmet desires. Traveling back one afternoon to the seminary where I taught two decades ago, I found a seat on the upper deck of a red London bus. Smoking was permitted "upstairs," so I usually chose seats below, but on this day they were all full. Maybe God wanted me "upstairs" that day, for as we journeyed south along the Old Kent Road, a sign painted high on a building caught my eye: CLUTCH CLINIC! It took a few moments for me to realize that the advertisement referred to an automobile service center specializing in the repair of defective clutches, for I heard the advertisement that day as God's invitation. "Supposing you spent time in my clutch clinic," God seemed to say. "What are some of the things you need to relinquish so that your hands can be open, ready to receive the grace I wait to give?" For the next few weeks I reflected on this challenge as it touched things, people, attitudes, desires, and expectations, recording in my journal the resistance to letting go, even as I longed for the will to do so.

Saint Benedict knew that God's word is spoken not only through scripture but also in the simple, ordinary events of each day. Attentiveness to the present moment as divine gift enables us to see and hear the Creator speak healing, forgiveness, joy, and hope, or to call our discipleship into question. At times, however, we become dull, sleepy, inattentive. In these moments God may startle and surprise us into awareness. My experience on that rainy British afternoon jolted me out of the inertia that had caused me to settle for mediocrity in prayer. Conversion was called for, and that required a painful scrutiny of the acquisitiveness that encumbers. As I began the process of letting God reveal the clutter, another image presented itself: I see myself as a five-year-old with a fistful of candy, which I am to share with my younger sister. But this is my candy, and I don't want her to have any of it, so my fingers close more tightly until all I have is a sticky, inedible mess. In God's clutch clinic, I began to name the stuff, long held but cloying, and to pray for clean, open hands.

The monastic community offered specific times for reflecting on the need for repentance, and Benedict offers a whole chapter on the twelve steps of humility, providing an excellent tool for recognizing our inclination to depart from God. When we allow God to draw us into seasons of personal examination and penitence, we are aided by the Spirit who will guide us "into all the truth" (John 16:13). To set out on a self-directed, critical evaluation that is not marinated in the grace of the gospel is to court hopelessness and depression.

So we begin our residence in the divine clutch clinic prayerfully, asking the Spirit to guide us; our first act of letting go is the acknowledgement that we cannot manage alone. In the context of a culture that encourages independence and autonomy, the desire to control all too easily dictates our actions, even our prayer. Asking for help is a first step in humility and conversion. It is a handing over of the unconscious arrogance that assumes if we work hard enough we can become who we are meant to be. By this willingness to let go we come to know with the mind of Christ and learn to walk with him into the recesses of heart and mind to clear out the clutter. Here the struggle begins, for we find ourselves very attached to what we have and very fearful of the changes we perceive as diminishment.

At the beginning of his ministry, Jesus retired to the barren hills of Judea for a period of reflection and preparation. In Mark's version of the temptation narrative (Mark 1:12-13), the Spirit drives Jesus into the wilderness, a strong declaration of being sent out or expelled suggesting divine necessity. In the time of testing that follows, Jesus is presented with choices that will either set him free to fulfill God's call or encumber him with a self-image dependent on the affirmation and deference of others. The clutch clinic of the Judean desert compels Jesus to relinquish the way of instant gratification, alignment with sociopolitical power structures, and self-aggrandizement. He returns to Galilee with open hands, ready to risk himself for God and to proclaim the gospel of repentance and forgiveness.

Saint Benedict left Rome and withdrew to a hillside cave above Lake Subiaco with the intention of listening to God and discerning God's call. Disgusted by the lifestyle practiced by many, aware of the breakdown of Western society and great political instability, he chose to anchor himself in a quiet place where at least one monk had preceded him. Little did he know that he would become "the father of Western monasticism" as his example drew others to a life of solitude and prayer and that his choice would burden him with heavy responsibility. Maybe like so many others drawn into the desert or onto rocky islands, he had to struggle with his desire to be left alone and finally accept his role as an instrument of God's grace through ministry to others.

My sense of being driven and compelled by the Spirit to remain in the place where my clutching would be challenged generated significant resistance. Yet in the struggles with self-will, an undergirding grace enabled me to uncurl tight fingers.

One of the first acts of letting go came as I prayed through my relationship with a colleague I had found difficult and toward whom I had become adversarial. The domineering rigidity I disliked in her had blinded me to her compassionate care for the seminarians. Now I began to recognize my own inclination toward control and inflexibility and the projection that enabled me to feel superior to her. I began to see and affirm her gifts and to find a new understanding of our commonality. Only when I released the desire to hold on to unexamined, critical judgments did God gift me with a loving appreciation for this woman. Over the next few weeks, my time in God's clutch clinic revealed many other pieces of clutter; the process of letting go continued. It continues today.

When some part of us is threatened, we easily begin to close our fingers around safe things. Frequently in his ministry Jesus faced the choice of speaking God's truth and risking hostility or compromising his message to gain acceptance. Many times he responded to people in need of healing, love, and affirmation when he longed for solitude and had every right to claim personal time. Often when asked to perform a miracle or to offer proof of his authority, he refused, knowing that spectacular signs that pander to publicity seekers can never be the hallmark of a ministry that points the way to God. The intensity of his desert struggles and the decisiveness of his response to God's call allowed Jesus to refuse temptations to clutch at power or opt for a self-image dependent on external recognition.

Likewise my time in the 1970s did not result in a once-for-all overcoming of my desire to hold on, but it did alert me to moments when I slip back into the old, fearful patterns. Fifteen years later I shared life in a monastery where the Rule of Saint Benedict pointed the way to simplicity and non-clinging. I found the wisdom of this sixth-century guide to

corporate living of the gospel stunningly relevant in our culture and context.

All Things in Common

In chapter 33 of the Rule, Benedict addresses the "evil practice"
of private ownership, demanding that the members uproot and
remove it from the monastery. The purpose of this instruction
is not deprivation. It is given so that every monk or sister might
grow in personal freedom and the community to which they
have committed their lives might be preserved. A deep sense of
the temporary nature of our earthly journey is embodied in the
relinquishing of claims to private ownership, having application far beyond the cloister. Today I own a house, a car, books,
a CD player, and many appliances that seem necessary to life
in our highly developed, fast-paced society. Does this chapter
of Benedict's Rule require that I let go of all these things? I think
not. Rather, it challenges me to consider what I mean when I
refer to them as "mine." It invites me to look to God, the source
of all that is, to express gratitude for the gifts I have been given,
and to know that they are temporarily loaned to me to be
enjoyed responsibly. I may not *cling* to them!

Saint Benedict speaks clearly about the tools and "goods" of
the monastery and insists that they be treated with respect. All
things in common use are to be cleaned carefully and replaced
after each use, a reminder that good order and stewardship of
things are as much a part of prayer as the chanting of psalms.
A monastic may not clutch at a particular hoe, book, or piece
of clothing but readily take what is given with gratitude for the
service of the community. I needed to remember this approach
when my turn came for kitchen duty in the monastery, and I
was tempted to take shortcuts or fail to sweep the floor.

One mosquito-laden day I remember walking past trash scattered at the back of the house. (Our location in the woods made raccoons frequent visitors for the tasty snacks inside the plastic garbage bags.) It wasn't "my" job to clean up the mess; several monks had come that way and had ignored it, so I felt fully justified in doing the same! "Whoever fails to keep the things belonging to the monastery clean or treats them carelessly should be reproved,"[2] says Saint Benedict; his words began to echo in my consciousness. It was time to stop clinging to a self-image that allowed me to separate myself from the common life that called me into love and service. Someone needed to pick up the trash and help keep the place clean. I was not required to be anywhere else at that moment, so with some reluctance I began to stuff the unsavory mess into a new plastic bag.

Then I had to address a more subtle inclination to clutch: It was all too easy to bask in self-righteous gratification because I had done what others ignored! Again Benedict seemed to whisper, "Your way of acting should be different from the world's way; the love of Christ must come before all else. You are not to act in anger or nurse a grudge. Rid your heart of all deceit."[3]

Could I pick up trash for the love of Christ without nursing a grudge against others? Could I willingly own the self-deception that so often went unnoticed even in the finest actions? Here was another clutch clinic moment through which God was calling me into a greater freedom and joy.

When the monastery closed about five years after I went to live there, a new, tough, letting-go time began. I'd learned to love the rhythm of monastic daily offices and Eucharist, the alone time in my hermitage, and the communal gatherings for meals and recreation. I interacted almost daily with guests who came for retreat. My job was to design workshops, expand the retreat ministry, and offer spiritual guidance. Now I was back "in the world" without a community or paid employment, and I was tempted to engage in nostalgic longing for what had been. "Let go!" God's word came and comes again and again as an invitation to embrace change, to stay alert, to wait for discernment, and then to receive the gifts of grace with open hands.

Often in his writings Paul draws a contrast between the first Adam, whose sinful grasping led to separation from God, and the second Adam, Christ, whose extended hands on the cross image the ultimate letting go. Someone has suggested that this typology may lie behind the hymn that Paul writes (or borrows) in his letter to the Philippians after he calls on his readers to have the mind of Christ (2:5-11). The hymn celebrates the total self-emptying of Christ and his choice of obedience to the Creator as he lets go of all claims to equality with God. If we read between the lines, we may discern the old Adam story recorded in Genesis. Inflated by a sense of his own importance, Adam grasped at the possibility of being like God, directly disobeying the divine word. The Philippians passage highlights two ways of living, two responses to a loving Creator. Paul says, "Choose the nongrasping way of Christ; let go; allow your hands to be open; have the mind of Christ" (AP).

The clutch clinic remains open. Saint Benedict offers his wisdom to twentieth-century Christians who live outside the cloister and struggle to be faithful to Christ by refusing the acquisitiveness of a culture that exalts grasping over letting go. Saint Paul continues to hold before us the need to choose the mind of Christ instead of the self-inflation that closes our fingers round sticky candy clutter. God, the gracious, attentive, expert mechanic of the soul, most deeply desires that we become whole, so we can celebrate the spaciousness of a world where all is gift. Yes, we have enough, and Saint Benedict will teach us more about our abundance as we reflect on his teaching.

Seeking Silence

The present day is witnessing a revival of interest in Saint Benedict and the wisdom of his teaching, perhaps in part because of the many parallels between his time and ours. An awareness of his context and history can help us make even greater connections with his teaching and its relevance to life now. Born around 480 C.E. in Nursia, central Italy, Benedict received his education in Rome but grew disillusioned by the decadent lifestyle of his contemporaries. Abandoning his studies he withdrew to a cave in the hills above Lake Subiaco and embraced a solitary, silent life. His solitude was short lived, however, as others, also disgusted by the morals and manners of the time, joined him. A monastic community began to evolve. After a few years Benedict and his monks moved further south to Monte Cassino, where they established a monastery, and the Rule was written to guide the community in its developing life.

Benedict lived in a time of great change and turmoil. A massive migration of "barbarian" tribes from the north during the fourth and fifth centuries challenged the more sophisticated Roman way of life and led to considerable political instability. As agrarian, uneducated peoples vied for land and displaced residents, a breakdown in western society inevitably occurred. Attempts to subdue the invaders and make them slaves in Roman households were largely unsuccessful, and the land fared better where they were allowed to become independent farmers. People lived in fear of war or rebellion; and shortly before Benedict's birth, the Gothic chieftain Theodoric defeated the last Western Roman emperor and assumed power. Instability, change, and a multicultural society generated deep unrest and a questioning of values.

In the cosmopolitan city of Rome, which Benedict left in disgust, child slavery and prostitution were commonplace; people in power unscrupulously used public office to increase their own wealth, and the gap between rich and poor widened radically. Violence, dishonest business practices, oppression and injustice characterized society. In places of learning, students vied for academic recognition while pursuing a life characterized by womanizing, drinking, vandalizing, and opulent banqueting.

So what's new?!

The church did not remain untouched by the prevailing culture. In 498 c.e. two rival candidates claimed the papacy, and though the church in Rome continued to exert major influence, local practices and worship became much more diverse. During the fourth and fifth centuries christological debates abounded as church councils made decisions about the nature of Christ and defined heresies, but theological conflicts continued throughout Benedict's lifetime, especially those relating to the nature of grace. There was much divergence of opinion, and those who held power in the church often were disconnected from the needs and questions of most believers. What emerged from Benedict's uncompromising withdrawal to seek God in solitude and prayer was a Rule that offered guidelines steeped in scripture for ordinary people living ordinary lives in every time.

Today many people hunger for a quiet place where they can reflect, seek God, and discern truth that will guide them on their life journey. Sadly some have turned to alternatives because they have not found in the Christian churches of their childhood and youth places for silence that honor deep questions and desires. Others have sought refuge in the fundamentalism that permeates most religious traditions and provides a rigid framework of belief that discourages questions and renders the quest for truth obsolete. Benedict invites us by his example and teaching to choose silence and solitude within the context of a Christian community that supports the quest for truth. He opens his Rule with these words: "Listen carefully, my son, to the master's instructions, and attend to them with the ear of your heart." The invitation to listen to the abbot is extended in the Rule to other members of the community and to the daily round of experience.

Whether monastics listen to scripture, the chanting of psalms, a community discussion, a pot boiling in the kitchen, or their own inner questions, they are to do so prayerfully, with the expectation that God's voice is heard in daily experience. Listening with the ear of the heart calls for attentiveness and an openness to the gentle whispers of divine grace. This concept is beautifully illustrated by several medieval artists seeking to represent the annunciation as Mary's listening heart responding to God's word spoken through Gabriel. A fine example is on display in the Cloisters Gallery, New York. The artist Robert Campin paints Mary seated on the floor—symbolic of her humility—reading scripture and not yet aware of Gabriel's presence. From a window high up on the wall a beam of light enters the room, slanting toward Mary's ear. Sliding down the sunbeam is a baby Jesus who carries a cross. This altarpiece, known as the Merode Triptych, was designed for meditation, inviting the viewer to adopt Mary's posture. Mary is impregnated through her ear; she hears God's word, and Jesus takes form within her.

We receive the Word as we listen not just with our ears but in the deepest places of our being. "Listen with the ear of your heart," says Benedict, the abbot, who longs to see Christ formed in his monks and so writes the Rule to guide them. His words echo those of Saint Paul: "My little children, for whom I am again in the pain of childbirth until Christ is formed in you, I wish I were present with you now" (Gal. 4:19-20). This book is designed to offer guidance for such groups so that they become hospitable circles of inclusivity that welcome all truth seekers, even those who have given up the church.

Political instability and crumbling world powers challenge us today, while our multicultural society compels us to expand our vision of God's commonwealth. We hear the voices of the dispossessed; the cries of abused children; the groans of the homeless, addicted, exploited, and disenfranchised neighbors. We must respond. Our times of silence and solitude become an essential factor in listening for the good news that God speaks to us through Christ. Only then may we discern ways in which God calls us to proclaim the good news to others through word, gesture, and action as we welcome them into the circle. In every face we learn to see Christ and, as Benedict instructs, to allow others to bless us by their presence in our midst.

Almost every news broadcast reveals new examples of persons in public office or corporate power using their positions for personal gain. We no longer trust our political leaders; we see an ever-widening chasm between those who make obscene salaries and single-parent families where hungry children without medical coverage are all too often seduced into the world of drugs, violence, and pornography. We are angry; we feel compassion; we know we must act even as disillusionment and despair threaten to engulf us, and here too Benedict's example guides us. Out of silent truth-seeking will come clarity about how and where our response as servants of Christ will take place.

Hildegard of Bingen, a later Benedictine, became one of the great prophets of the twelfth century. She embraced the justice-making mandate of Christian faith by challenging political and religious leaders of her time. She even told the pope to wake up, to cut out the roots of evil, and to cease tolerating corrupt men who pollute the truth! Withdrawal into monastic silence is not an evasion of the world's problems but a decision as to where we choose to draw our power to act. "Listen" says Saint Benedict "and then labor to do what God asks."[4]

Our time resembles Benedict's also as we see the church in turmoil, often tempted to clutch at old "certainties," unwilling to engage in the painful struggle to embrace fresh insights. Currently issues of gender, sexual orientation, ethnicity, and clerical abuse of the pastoral relationship occupy the agenda of several denominational bodies. How do we decide our response to these questions? All too often the divisive way of engaging in acrimonious debate, each side claiming to have the truth, results in a power play in which there are winners and losers. Neither side "hears" the other; the goal is to prevail, not to listen. Benedict requires that his community members listen with respect to one another, paying attention even to the youngest, rookie monk who may well have an important contribution from his recent experience in the world.

Saint Benedict, a man for all seasons, a teacher, a listener, and a spiritual guide, preferred Christ above all else and immersed himself in scripture. He teaches us that prayer takes place as much in the fields, kitchen, and marketplace as in the church or cloister. He offers practical guidance about food, work, relationships, rest, recreation, and leadership. We find the stability we crave when God is at the center of our personal and community life and when we take time to be still and listen. Benedict invites us to dig deep, to lay firm foundations in the bedrock of faith and prayer, so that the storm seasons of our lives cannot dislodge us.

ONE

PRAYING THE SCRIPTURES

❦

Listen readily to holy reading,
and devote yourself often to prayer.[1]

FOR THE PSALMIST, God's word was the source of delight. The image of healthy, young, green trees planted by water that feeds their root system is used of those whose "delight is in the law of the Lord" (Ps. 1:2). The writer of Psalm 119, the longest psalm, speaks of delight in scripture on at least ten occasions and uses many metaphors to celebrate the richness of God's law. Scripture is a treasure; it sets the heart free; it brings light and peace; it is sweeter than honey and becomes like songs even in places where the psalmist is not at home. This love for God's word also permeates the Rule of Saint Benedict, which is saturated by biblical quotations and provides daily time for public reading and private reflection on scripture. The frequent chanting of the Psalter offered a rhythm for monastic communities not unlike the continual breaking of waves on the seashore.

The Hebrew/Christian scriptures were primary reading, so the monks came to know the content of the Bible well. Through their community life of worship, study, and following the Rule, the monks applied the lessons of scripture. In personal times of prayer each monk practiced that heart listening to the word that shaped his own spiritual formation. The Benedictine model of scriptural reflection, *lectio divina* (holy reading), allows the biblical text to touch our lives today in a rich, insightful way.

A Personal Story

I spent my own formative years in an Evangelical Free Church in England, which revered the Bible as the authoritative, inerrant word of God. Sunday sermons were long and heavily biblical, and all serious church members were expected to be present at the weekly Bible study. The church permitted no critical study of the text, a method represented as a blasphemous approach to the sacred scriptures. Interpretation, drawing its inspiration from John Calvin and the Puritans, was rigidly conservative. The result of this formation was threefold. I found in biblical fundamentalism an authoritative support system and certainty in matters of faith constructed on an infallible Bible. I learned to know the scriptures well and immersed myself in serious study of the text. And I learned to love these writings and the God I perceived through them.

I am deeply grateful to those who nurtured in me this knowledge of the scriptures. My faith journey has led me to relinquish biblical fundamentalism, but my love for the Bible is like an intoxicant. New insights constantly surprise me as I ask the Holy Spirit to guide my reading, and I discover a constant shattering of the inadequate images in which I construct the Creator. For God is Mystery, inviting me in these sacred pages to take off my shoes and stand silent on this holy ground. God is always beyond my imagining while remaining inexplicably present, infusing me with hunger for the word that gives life.

Seminary plunged me into the world of academic theology; biblical criticism was the prerequisite for university graduation. At first I tried the ostrich approach; I managed pretty easily at the start. I really believed the truth of my earlier teachers and seriously doubted that the academic theologians favored truth. I managed to suppress doubts when the results of critical analysis seemed more plausible to me than literalism; and as a result, the schizophrenic syndrome between religious upbringing and the world of academia began. It lasted several years, at one time almost resulting in an abandonment of faith altogether. Only when I could readily face the fear of loss—loss of certainty, external affirmation, an infallible Bible, and a cherished support system—did the idols begin to shatter. This period of darkness, disorientation, and doubt paradoxically became a time in which I knew that God *is* more profoundly than ever before.

I could no longer claim with integrity the inerrancy of the Bible, yet the essential truth of the scriptures became more alive and real as I let go of fear. Gone was the need for intellectual gymnastics to "prove" that God created the world in six days. The two different and sometimes conflicting stories of creation in the opening chapters of Genesis yielded far richer meaning as I allowed them to speak for themselves without imposing twentieth-century scientific analysis upon them. Now I found a loving God smiling as each new phase of creation took place and saying, "Behold, it is very good." This God, who celebrates the wonder of all that is made, including man and woman created together in the divine image, also gave to them stewardship of the earth.

The newness of such an insight, the wonder and responsibility of it, exploded into my consciousness and then into my prayers. Because of this insight I could no longer passively observe the rape of the earth, the inequitable distribution of its produce, or the oppression of many of its people. This God involved me in an ongoing process of caring for and redeeming the world so that once again the proclamation, "Behold, it is very good," might be made. Such prayerful and praiseful response never came from endless debates defending God against the scientists. Unwittingly I was beginning to practice *lectio divina,* although I had not yet even heard the term.

Academic study of the New Testament taught me there is no guarantee that we have, verbatim, the words of Jesus. After all, no one was around with a tape recorder when the first Gospel came into written form some twenty-five years after the death of Jesus. We have inherited the accounts of the life and teaching of Jesus written by persons whose lives he transformed. They wrote from a post-Resurrection perspective and after years of reflection. By that time some of their confusion about Jesus had cleared. They had come to know the Christ of faith, to live their way into the teaching of the historical Jesus, and to discover the enduring quality of his life. They recorded the words they remembered and those preserved through the oral tradition. They recorded the essential, life-changing message of Jesus, not out of a Western compulsion for linguistic accuracy but from the experience of being transformed by it. Transformation is Benedict's aim too.

I began to read the gospel not out of fear because the inerrant words of Christ had been taken from me but believing that the eternal Word speaks in and beyond the written account. "Who do people say that I am?" Jesus asks his disciples at Caesarea Philippi, and they offer a variety of conjectures—John the Baptist, Elijah, one of the prophets. "But who do you say that I am?" They must make their own response, confess him, and subsequently come to understand the less palatable dimensions of the statement of faith. Peter answers for them, "You are the Messiah," and soon they hear that even this answer is incomplete; their understanding of the nature of messiahship is inadequate. They want glory, but Jesus will manifest his glory through suffering. By the time the Gospel writers record the story, they have learned for themselves that discipleship is not a comfortable option. As I read the story I hear the question in my own time and context: "Who do you say that I am?" Biblical criticism has not robbed me of the voice of God. Instead I am compelled to search for my own answer and to relinquish the projections I make of a comfortable Christ figure who will not disturb me. I need to say who Jesus is for me again and again, at ever-deepening levels of experience.

Dealing with Obstacles ——

Because our past experience conditions our approach to the scriptures, it is helpful to reflect on the people and traditions that have shaped our understanding of the Bible. If our primary source of information has been preaching or teaching by "experts," we may need to confront the fear of coming to the sacred text ourselves without their expertise. Many of the monks of Benedict's day were illiterate. They heard scripture read by those more educated, and they memorized passages that could be reflected on later. Benedict states that the "heart listening" he insists upon in the Rule is open to all and expected of all. We need not fear lack of education or the absence of theologians to instruct, for the spirit of God who inspired the divine writings will teach us. Benedict, with the author of Deuteronomy, would say to us, "The word is very near to you; it is in your mouth and in your heart for you to observe" (30:14).

Some Christians who have attended church for many years

come to the Bible with a sense of inadequacy because they know little about it. They may remember a few favorite texts like Psalm 23 or the Sermon on the Mount, but the relationship among and context of historical books, prophets, gospels, and epistles are unknown. It seems a daunting task to acquire the knowledge necessary to understand the scriptures. Again the Rule is helpful. In Benedict's community, time was given for study and a more systematic approach to holy scripture and other writings but not as a prerequisite to letting God speak through a text or verse of the Bible. Accurate, academic dissection of the material was not the primary aim of being with the word. Instead the approach was to sit quietly in the presence of God and with open heart and mind to wait until the text touched a deep place within and invited the listener into conversation with its Author. None of us needs fear lack of knowledge as we come to scripture in this simple, expectant way.

There are some who may have to overcome an experience of having the Bible used as a weapon to make them conform. A woman whom I will call Mary told me of her great fear of scripture and of the angry God behind it, a view inherited from childhood. She was raised in a strict home where the Bible was read daily at mealtimes and used to control behavior. Her clergyman father was a strict disciplinarian who believed (and quoted) scripture to justify frequent and humiliating beatings (Prov. 13:24). She learned that God was always watching, not to bless and enfold but to catch her out and punish her for every tiny misdemeanor. Now married to a clergyman, she is learning to love and be loved by God and to hear scripture as good news for each moment.

Benedict's community included some who had been slaves, children, and undoubtedly those who were damaged by the powers of the church. Although he does not address them with the psychological terms we might use today in dealing with abuse or fear, Benedict does insist that the abbot treat each monk individually. The uniqueness of each person and his or her experience of life does not get left outside the monastery gate. People enter community bringing their past with them, and formation takes place as they consent to the process of growing into God and dealing with old wounds and fears.

In some cases theological training, biblical criticism, exegesis, and homiletics—all components in the training of clergy—can impede the ability to read scripture devotionally. Seminary is a melting pot where the serious challenge of assimilating new approaches to biblical literature is a severe one, sometimes leading to a faith crisis. The discovery that one has built faith on shaky foundations can shatter the often hard-won struggle to accept a vocation to ministry. Theological training raises questions, uncovers paradoxes, and increases ambiguity. The resulting spiritual confusion hurts. If, instead of refusing loss of the illusion of certainty and fixed assumptions, we consent to this process of stripping that places our faith in question, we learn to know God who is Mystery.

Critical analysis of the scriptures and their devotional use need not conflict with each other. The author of John's Gospel tells us that Jesus said, "I am the truth," and that his purpose was to lead us into all truth. We need not fear losing the truth if we allow the insights of current scholarship to challenge our interpretation of the Bible. We may feel uncomfortable at times; we may not like what we learn if our cherished images are broken. But if we are willing to be confused, questioned, and stimulated into new ways of thinking, the scriptures will become even more alive to us. Personally I found the movement from disintegration to synthesis to be painful, prolonged, and richly rewarding. I was blessed with a wise guide who helped me through the confusion and questions and who did not minimize the struggle. Often he encouraged me to stay in it, to wait and trust instead of trying to short-circuit the confusion. Saint Benedict too placed wise monks in mentoring positions for those new to the formation process and called upon the abbot to shepherd those in his care.

Sometimes older versions of the Bible with which we have become familiar can be an obstacle in the way of fresh insights. Those familiar with the King James Version of the Bible will recall that in his farewell discourses (John 14–17) Jesus promised to send "another Comforter" to be with the disciples after his departure. Today's reader might entertain warm, contented feelings when reading that passage. Yet the translators of this version had no such thoughts. In the seventeenth century a comforter was a goad, a means of prodding reluctant servants or animals into action. So in this translation, the Holy Spirit comes not as the bringer of peace and tranquility in Jesus' absence but as a disturbing, insistent spur that presses the disciples into action. Using a new or different Bible translation, especially one with which we are unfamiliar, may be a means of grace as well-known words or phrases are replaced with new ones that jolt us into fresh insight. There is nothing static about the Rule of Saint Benedict, and there are no limits to God's desire to address us through the written word. We respond to the invitation to listen with the ears of our hearts by coming faithfully to the word each day and setting aside assumptions, fears, and prejudice as we allow God to surprise us with good news.

God's Word in Contemporary Life

An important, fresh approach to biblical interpretation has emerged among Third World Christians, especially those in

Latin America. Liberation Theology, as it is called, is a process of setting people free from the constraints of oppression whether they be religious, political, or racial. The primary concern centers around *orthopraxis*, a term that means to work out and practice the implications of Christian faith. The question is less "What do you believe?" and more "How do you live?" Right conduct is crucial. Perhaps greater support for *orthopraxis* (right practice) will help overcome reticence about engaging with the scriptures. Today's Liberation Theology is closely akin to *lectio divina*.

The abstract approach of much Western theology has little appeal for the poor and oppressed in Latin America. They are not much interested in the various arguments for the existence of God that occupied many seminary hours for most clergy. Instead they are concerned about having enough to eat, a decent place to live, and the dignity of human labor. Most do not have an advanced education and many are illiterate, so the question of reading and interpreting the Bible "correctly" is difficult. For many the church has lost credibility because of its seemingly strong association with a wealthy oligarchy and its offer to redress the imbalances of society only in an afterlife. It seems to have done little to alleviate present suffering, and the hungry cannot eat platitudes. Out of the soil of inequity Liberation Theology has grown, and people have begun to learn that the gospel of Jesus Christ is about freedom and justice. What is more, they have begun to realize that they can be involved in bringing about such ideals.

Highly contextual, Liberation Theology begins with an analysis of society and goes on to ask how the scriptures relate to the status quo. In Latin America people observed that a small number of very wealthy people held power over a growing number of poor. It also became obvious that most commodities, including theology, were imported and therefore foreign. Aid and investment from wealthy countries often resulted in job losses for the peasant farmers, profits going to the multinational companies who came to "help." Did the scriptures have anything to say that could give hope in this situation?

In order to respond to this question, intentional communities began to form and to study the Bible from their own perspective. The priest no longer functioned as the authority figure who had the answers, telling people how and what to believe. Instead the priest became the facilitator of a process in which each person learned to *do* theology. Often biblical accounts were being heard for the first time, and there was an air of excitement as people made their own connections with the text.

Even well-known stories took on a new dimension. The poor, beaten down by their own society, could identify with the beaten person lying by the side of the road. A priest and Levite passed by, but only a despised Samaritan offered help. Those who might be expected to help, respected leaders with resources, ignored the plight of the victim. Who then was the helper? The the compassionate one was himself despised and marginalized by society, and it was easy for the poor of Latin America to see themselves in the Samaritan. They could support and help one another by coming together and expressing solidarity as they pooled their resources. The gospel gave them an impetus for self-help, and cooperatives of various kinds sprang out of their reading and applying the scriptures.

Such application of the gospel is *orthopraxis*—right action to alleviate distress and resist oppression. Like the Israelites leaving bondage in Egypt, the poor of Latin America hear the word of the Lord, which enables them to let go of passivity and hopelessness and to claim their freedom.

It would be inappropriate for those of us living outside Latin

America simply to take over the conclusions of Liberation Theology in that society. Our task is to engage with the same seriousness in an analysis of our own society and then allow the scriptures to address us where we are. Simply to discover what they meant in the days of Jesus will not do. It is possible to be a highly skilled academic theologian, an expert in exegesis, without making application of the Bible to daily life. Equally the person who has received little or no Bible training can relate the message of the scriptures to contemporary situations in the most insightful way, given encouragement and support.

True education consists in the drawing out and validation of the wisdom deep within each person, precisely what Saint Benedict encourages as he affirms the uniqueness of each monk. When we allow for the innate capacity to make connections, when we share insight instead of locating wisdom in a few experts to whom we give power and authority, then community building can begin and we will hear the liberating gospel in our time and place.

The Benedictine approach to the Bible, known as *lectio divina*, also alleviates some of the difficulties we experience when we try to read a document written in a vastly different time and culture. Making connections with the scriptures and our own experience often leads to a desire to dig into the historical and exegetical background in order to understand more fully and respond more effectively. But such investigation is not a prerequisite. Rather, the energy for further examination flows from a sense of the contemporary nature of the scriptures and their importance for our lives. It does not take a farmer or theologian to make sense of the parable of the sower. We find ourselves in the old image as we ponder Jesus' words.

The word of God is the seed scattered on the soil of human lives. Sometimes it falls upon the hard pathway, where it cannot take root and the birds of busy-ness, fatigue, and boredom consume it. As a result we do not pray the Bible because its treasure is quickly snatched from us. It has only briefly touched the hard parts of our lives. Sometimes the word of God falls in the shallow places, and though our enthusiasm may cause an initial growth, it loses its effectiveness quickly. The seed dies because we resist the effort to dig deep in order to get beyond the hard core of bedrock, opting instead for superficial religious experience. The weeds that we are unwilling to uproot will strangle some seed with their tendrils. God's truth and our unreality may look deceptively similar, but ultimately one of them will die. Sometimes we may be deceived into imagining that the weeds we cultivate are essentials of faith, while God invites us to uproot them so that in the darkness of uncertainty the real seed can grow.

But the gospel tells us that some seed will fall on soil well prepared, on good earth filled with nutrients. Any gardener will confirm that time, study, and effort are required before the ground is ready to receive the seed that will grow into a harvest. And Jesus conveys this understanding when he tells this powerful little parable about the living word of God. All four possibilities exist in each of us; how we receive the word will determine how we pray it. God's purpose is harvest. Our response to the seed gift is part of the divine-human cooperation in a world alive with possibility. God relies on us to be part of that cosmic movement toward wholeness and fulfillment that will reach its consummation when the whole created order is brought under the authority of Christ. To this end we are to hear, live, and pray the scriptures.

Practicing Lectio Divina

The ancient Christian art of *lectio divina* promotes the listening to and relating of scripture to this moment in our experience. Choose a time of day when you are alert and relaxed and select a quiet, restful place. It may come as a surprise to consider alertness and relaxation together, since we often associate being alert with strain or effort and being relaxed with inactivity. However, in most great religious traditions paying attention or being alert is a fundamental prerequisite for prayer, and relaxing body and mind promotes rather than hinders attentiveness. I usually begin my prayer time with some simple stretching exercises to awaken my body and to become aware of my physical being as "a living sacrifice, holy and acceptable to God, which is your spiritual worship" (Rom. 12:1). Then I assume a comfortable posture and pay attention to my breath, slowly relaxing each limb and allowing my breathing rhythm to help quiet my mind.

A quiet, restful place is important too; and if you do not already have such a special area where you pray, you might choose to create one. It does not require a lot of space. A candle, an icon, a cross, objects from nature, or other special items that help you focus on prayer can make the space inviting. When you are settled and still, pray for the Holy Spirit's guidance as you enter this time of prayer. Begin to follow the steps below, aware that they are not stages in an orderly process but a means through which the inner rhythms of our spirit become more in tune, more filled with the presence of God.

Beware of judging your prayer by the quality of the *lectio* or by how long or short a time you spend on each step. Sometimes you may read a passage of scripture, and a word or phrase will immediately touch you, striking a powerful note that resonates with your experience and bringing you into a harmony of gratitude or adoration. Let it be. Remain thankful in contemplation if this is where you are; do not worry about missed steps. If your prayer seems to be hard work and nothing much emerges, commit to faithful follow-through with the steps and let the disappointment or impatience become a place out of which you pray.

Step 1: READING *(lectio).* Slowly and gently read the scriptures, savoring and staying with words or phrases that speak to the depths of your heart. Listen to the word "with the ear of your heart" and be willing to stay with portions of the text that address you in a special way. You might think of this step as "loitering with intent"; that is, through repetition allowing the text to linger in your memory to the end that you are able to receive the gift God holds out to you through this passage. You may want to set aside the printed text and listen in quietness to the word that has already touched your heart.

Step 2. MEDITATION *(meditatio—rumination).* Like the ruminant that chews the cud to extract all the rich nutrition from its food, repeat and ponder the text you have internalized until it yields its savor. Allow the scripture passage to interact with your memories, hopes, and concerns. If distractions arise ask yourself if they are leading you off at a tangent (in which case simply acknowledge their presence and let them go) or if they offer a further insight into the text. Distracting thoughts that need to be remembered later can be jotted down so that you do not spend the rest of the prayer time wondering if you will recall them when you are done! Keep gently coming back to the text when you are drawn away by conflicting thoughts.

Step 3. PRAYER *(oratio).* Now let the text call you to place your whole being before God. Let the word you have heard become a word of offering, dedication, and desire in which you give to God your deepest longings and concerns. Allow dialogue to take place as you respond to God who has already addressed you through the inspired word and who, through the scriptures, draws you deeper into the divine presence. You may write this dialogue in your journal to remind you of the conversation, or you may choose to record a brief description of the experience at the end of your prayer time.

Step 4. CONTEMPLATION *(contemplatio).* When you are ready, simply rest silently in the presence of God without words. Be willing to let go of the scripture that has led you into the divine presence and allow yourself to enjoy communion with our loving Creator God who stands behind and is known through the scriptures. Saint Benedict reassures us and invites us into joy as he encourages us to go on: "As we progress in this way of life and in faith, we shall run on the path of God's commandments, our hearts overflowing with the inexpressible delight of love."[2]

A JOURNAL ENTRY

January 19, 1995

"Those who wait for me shall not be put to shame" (Isa. 49:23).

Waiting for God—how hard it is! This seems to come as a word not to rush things but to try in each decision to discern God's purpose. Today's psalm (50) has God speaking to the covenant people and to those who "refuse discipline," and the emphasis is on offering a sacrifice of thanksgiving. My prayer began with gratitude for many blessings as I watched rhododendron leaves move gently in the rain. Accepting the discipline of waiting with attention is the invitation from scripture for today.

WORD OF GOD, you speak in silence and in the midst of each day's work. Sometimes I try to tune you out by replacing listening with many busy things. May your truth, proclaimed in scripture, find a home in my heart, always recalling me to grateful living and childlike trust. Amen.

SUGGESTIONS FOR REFLECTION

1. Take some time to create (or enhance) the special place where you will pray, read, and journal each day.

2. Begin practicing *lectio divina* by reading Mark 1:35-39. If you do not already keep a journal, begin today by writing down your reflections on this passage.

3. Think back over your experience with scripture, including childhood memories. What attitudes, joys, fears emerge? Who were your teachers/mentors? What old messages might you relinquish or new blessings might you embrace? What obstacles do you notice today as you become more intentional about daily *lectio divina*? Pondering these questions and writing your responses may help clear the way for heart listening.

TWO

HOSPITALITY

❦

Your way of acting should be
different from the world's way; the love of Christ
must come before all else. You are not to act in anger
or nurse a grudge. Rid your heart of all deceit.
Never give a hollow greeting of peace or turn
away someone who needs your love.[1]

IN 1985 I LEFT the noise and hustle of New York City and moved
to the South Carolina Low Country. After the crazed pace of life
in the Big Apple as one of six priests on staff at a large midtown
parish, I found myself surrounded by swamps, cows, mosqui-
toes, and monks! And it all came about because of a love affair.
The affair began several years earlier when I met Benedict and
heard him address me in my time and place even though his
voice echoed through fourteen centuries. I fell in love because
this man spoke of life in a hospitable community; of simplicity,
balance, and an ordered way of living designed to create an environment that fosters freedom to grow fully into the persons God
created us to be. When the Order of the Holy Cross invited me
to become a monastic oblate and to share its life at Holy Savior
Priory in Pineville, South Carolina, I felt ready. For five years I
experienced the reality of community life, its joys and struggles,
growth and stagnation, the foibles and vulnerabilities of those

who lived together under a common rule. The Rule of Benedict was read daily and, together with scripture, formed the bedrock on which the community was built. I found Benedict's teachings staggeringly relevant to contemporary life and relationships, uncomfortably challenging at times, and always pulling us back to the centrality of Christ when we got sidetracked onto our own agendas. The Priory closed in 1991, but the affair continues.

Now I face the challenge of interpreting the wisdom of Saint Benedict without the daily support of a residential community. Each day I try to be an attentive learner in the school for God's service, and Benedict continues to guide me on my faith journey and to invite me to create a space in which I welcome all "as Christ." Now I need to ask, "Is my home truly a place of hospitality?" and to allow the Rule to remind me that the office, grocery store, and neighborhood offer ample opportunity to greet others in this hospitable way.

God's hospitality as a loving Creator who calls us into relationship and gives generously to fulfill our deepest longings became the model for Benedictine community life and for extending welcome to strangers. Private ownership was relinquished and every possession regarded as gift, received in order to be shared with others. Benedict made it clear that people do not enter our lives to be coerced or manipulated but to enrich us by their differences and to be received graciously in the name of Christ. His guidelines continue to suggest ways in which our homes and church communities can become places of profound Christian hospitality today.

Hospitality in Creation

The Rule of Benedict is steeped in scripture and in the awareness that all things come from God and belong to God. At creation God blessed everything that had been made and entrusted the earth and all its creatures to humankind. A second creation story employs the image of a fruitful garden, a place of hospitality, in which people are invited to live harmoniously in communion with the creator God who has loved them into being. The monastery is designed to become a microcosm of that garden, where God is given the first place in human affections, where people love one another, where a disciplined life enables all to enter into joy and gratitude and to serve God. God's generous hospitality gives rise to attentive care for all things in the Rule of Benedict.

> The goods of the monastery, that is, its tools, clothing or anything else, should be entrusted to the brothers whom the abbot appoints and in whose manner of life he has confidence....Whoever fails to keep the things belonging to the monastery clean or treats them carelessly should be reproved.[2]

The monastic community recognizes everything as gift and therefore worthy of respect; members of the community are welcome guests in God's world, not owners who exploit it. When the brothers work in the fields, their labor is no less sacred than their singing in the choir; the farm implements deserve the same honor given to altar vessels. The order equips the monks going on a journey with stronger footwear and newer clothing, serviceable garments that will be laundered and placed back in the wardrobe when they return. No one owns anything privately; all is on temporary loan and therefore demands care and attention.

This aspect of Benedict's teaching seems especially timely as we deal with the results of human exploitation of the environment. We are guests in God's world and stewards of its resources, called upon to treat with reverence all that God gives to enhance life. Our commitment to reduce waste, recycle, and reuse when possible evidences our gratitude to the Creator and our respect for others. The Rule also challenges the acquisitiveness of our culture. Benedict speaks to me powerfully in my life outside the cloister; in fact, sometimes the greater challenge comes in letting go of the desire to have, to control, and to guard what has been given as though it were mine alone. As I try to share what I have, to treat goods with reverence, and to live out of gratitude, I glimpse the freedom that comes from living by trusting the generosity of the Creator. Benedict encourages me to live as a respectful guest in this wonderful world God has made.

Many people today speak of a yearning for community. Sometimes even churches lack the dynamic sense of belonging and sharing that characterized Jesus' teaching and the experience of the first Christians: "Now the whole group of those who believed were of one heart and soul, and no one claimed private ownership of any possessions, but everything they owned was held in common" (Acts 4:32). Community breaks down when "mine" replaces "ours," when we no longer regard what we have as a gracious gift through which we bless others. Benedict challenges us to consider how we can share our "goods" and at the same time invites us to examine our motivations for acquiring more. One friend of mine responds by pressing the mute button on her TV control each time commercials interrupt a program. Perhaps a question that will help us in our decision making about acquiring things might be, "How will this enable me to live as a hospitable guest in God's world and support the community of faith?"

The harmony of the garden, as we all know, was soon interrupted by a discordant note as an attitude of mistrust and grasping slithered in through the bushes. Deception, blame, lying, and the desire to hide from the consequences of their actions destroyed the blissful relationship of Adam and Eve with each other and God. The same thing happened in the early Christian community when a couple sold a piece of property and brought a portion of the proceeds to the apostles. It appears that they wanted to be respected for their generosity and represented their gift at the full-sale value. Ananias and Sapphira could freely choose what to do with their money, but an attitude of acquisitiveness caused them to lie with disastrous consequences for them and a painful loss to the community.

Benedict was no idealist. He knew only too well that when people live together tensions arise; relationships break down. If not addressed promptly, these tensions will poison the life of the community. There is much in the Rule to guide us in terms of the everyday business of living together, of honoring the Christ in one another even as we recognize our ability to hurt those we love. The three vows—stability, conversion of life, and obedience—translate readily into guidelines for our life together in the present.

Vows Leading to Hospitality

The vow of stability relates to the monk's commitment to remain in the monastery serving Christ in the brothers and guests unless the community sends him out on a mission. This commitment is in contrast to some restless, itinerant beggars who abuse the hospitality of others and live without discipline. Benedict has harsh words to say about the "gyrovagues, who spend their entire lives drifting from region to region, staying as guests for three or four days in different monasteries. Always on the move, they never settle down, and are slaves to their own wills and gross appetites."[3] The vow of stability affirms sameness, a willingness to attend to the present moment, to the reality of this place, and to these people as God's gift to us and the setting where we live out our discipleship. We are discouraged from fantasizing some ideal situation in which we will finally be able to pray and live as we should. Instead Benedict says, "Be here; find Christ in the restless teenager, demanding parent, insensitive employer, dull preacher, lukewarm congregation. Resist the inclination to rush out and find some new recipe for happiness or the spiritual shot in the arm offered by television evangelists or a different church community because it is reputed to have more exciting worship." Commitment to stability affirms the "sacrament of the present moment"[4] and enables us to create a hospitable space for whomever and whatever God sends into our lives *now*.

Being in the present moment is no easy task, especially when we are interrupted by someone who needs our attention at a crucial time in some project. But attentiveness is what stability asks of us; this is how we express hospitality as we let go of what we are doing and pay attention to the person who needs our love. Hospitable stability says yes to the present moment whether it brings discomfort or joy, boredom or excitement, because it always offers us the opportunity to welcome the Christ presence into consciousness and to refuse an easy escape into the fantasy world of self-fulfillment. We can only be fully ourselves when we know who we are as members of the community of faith, serving one another in partnership with God. Stability does not imply a static response to life, however.

The second vow, conversion of life, makes it clear that dealing with change is also essential. By this vow the monk recognizes that he is not yet fully the person God created him to be, that he is on the way to knowing himself as one loved and created in the divine image, whose call is to be as Christ in the world but who has not yet arrived. The Rule makes provision for the weaknesses, failures, and foibles of members of the community. It deals with issues of repentance and forgiveness, of restoration to fellowship with the rest of the brothers, and of compassion toward those who fail. This conversion, *metanoia*, implies an ongoing inner transformation through which comfortable categories of thought and dearly held ways of doing things are challenged and relinquished for the greater good of the community. It involves the kind of iconoclasm that Dietrich Bonhoeffer speaks of in his book *Life Together* when he warns of the danger of setting a personal ideal of community above the community itself!5

Once again I find Benedict addresses contemporary life. We live our lives in the world, in families, and in churches where we often discover that we hurt others, judge them, let them down. Sometimes we try to manipulate or coerce people to satisfy our own needs instead of freeing them to be themselves. Sometimes, like the prodigal in the Gospel story, we take what we can get and use our resources wastefully until we discover our own poverty and the love we have despised. Then it is time to return home. It is time for conversion of life, for asking forgiveness and starting over. The vow of conversion of life is not about saving face but about accepting ourselves and accepting one another in all our humanness. Through forgiveness God accepts us, which is the essence of healthy community, one that fosters an atmosphere of openness, hospitality, and the possibility of change.

The third vow, obedience, may cause us to cringe as we recall teachers and parents who seemed to demand that we unquestioningly do their bidding. However, Benedict does not intend cowering submission. Obedience is first due to Christ who invites us to "listen with the ear of your heart" and then labor to do what is required. The abbot, as a "father who loves you," exercises leadership in such a way that each monk can listen to and discern God's way and then get on with it. Obedience lies in listening to and doing the will of God.

The monastery provides a structure and discipline in which this way of life may be lived, but monks are not required to act out of blind obedience to some mind-bending cult leader. The abbot models his gentleness, fairness, and wisdom—and his dealing with each monk according to his personality and needs—on the way of Christ with disciples. The centrality of scripture gives form to obedience. It is Christ that the monk, that we, hear; and it is Christ whom we share with others who hunger for love and acceptance.

Welcoming the Stranger

The sharing of Christian hospitality with strangers receives strong emphasis in the Rule. Benedict instructs that

> All guests who present themselves are to be welcomed as Christ, for he himself will say: I was a stranger and you welcomed me....Proper honor must be shown *to all*....Once a guest has been announced, the superior and the brothers are to meet him with all the courtesy of love....All humility should be shown in addressing a guest on arrival or departure. By a bow of the head or by a complete prostration of the body, Christ is to be adored because he is indeed welcomed in them....Great care and concern are to be shown in receiving poor people and pilgrims, because in them more particularly is Christ received.[6]

Benedict goes on to describe the characteristics of the person who serves as porter at the monastery gate. He is to be an older man chosen for his graciousness and wisdom, since he will be the first monk encountered by a stranger. When someone knocks the porter will call out, "Thanks be to God," or "Your blessing please." Then, "with all the gentleness that comes from the fear of God, he provides a prompt answer with the warmth of love."[7] Provision is made for the comfort of pilgrims, enabling them to enter into the peace and rhythm of the monastery and to receive sustenance on their journey. The monks give hospitality not out of a sense of superiority but with a willingness to receive whatever a guest might teach them. "Your blessing please" says, "I am glad you are here; I recognize Christ in you; I am ready to receive what you have to offer; I welcome you to this place to share our life."

The Rule wisely guides us as we try to be welcoming and inclusive. Benedict does not first ask that a visitor understand and conform to a belief system or social milieu. Instead persons are received as they are and invited into a place where acceptance and compassion generate the desire for God, for fullness of life. Benedict's way is the way of Christ, who welcomed without distinction and set before people a vision of what they might become.

This model of hospitality is illustrated most clearly in the story of the encounter between Jesus and the woman at the well (John 4:1-42). When Christ meets her that hot afternoon, his heart yearns with compassion for her as he senses her loneliness and need. By coming to draw water in the middle of the day she announces her alienation from others. No one went out in the heat to do chores but instead rested until later in the day. Jesus takes time to be aware of where she is and to be present to her, and he recognizes that she has something to give him. "Your blessing please," says the porter at the door of the monastery. "Please give me a drink of water," says Jesus to a woman whose life is arid.

The Samaritan woman expresses surprise; Jesus, a Jew, has spoken to her, a woman of despised race. Clearly he is no ordinary Jew, since he sets aside religious taboos, social expectations, and traditional gender behavior in order to affirm her. Both Benedict and Jesus teach us that our openness to receive from even the most needy also opens a door of hope for them. The woman's interest is aroused; and as they engage in conversation, her thirst for what this stranger embodies increases. Only when Jesus has dismissed irrelevant arguments about religion does he invite her to consider the emptiness of her life. Only then can he speak to her of the need for a new way of being and offer himself as the source of living water, that will never run dry. John 4:39-42 describes the result of this encounter:

> Many Samaritans from that city believed in him because of the woman's testimony.... So when the Samaritans came to him, they asked him to stay with them.... And many more believed because of his word. They said to the woman, "It is no longer because of what you said that we believe, for we have heard for ourselves, and we know that this is truly the Savior of the world."

This transforming encounter began with a simple act of hospitality. Jesus received with grace a person in need and allowed her to minister to him.

One of the guests at the monastery in South Carolina had been searching many years for a spiritual path. The man had tried various kinds of meditation, had visited numerous churches, and had spent time living in an Ashram in India. He came to spend a week with us, a little nervous about monks but ready to enter into the rhythm of life, even attending Matins at 5:30 each morning! In the course of conversation we learned that he loved to cook, so we invited him to prepare supper for the community and guests. This was not a contrived "need" that we invented to make him feel at home; with so few of us taking care of the place, his gift provided a welcome break for those of us who shared kitchen duties. He accepted the invitation with delight, and we enjoyed the superb meal he prepared. As the week went on, he began to relax and finally went away having found the faith he was seeking. "Your blessing please; your gift; please share with us what you have to offer as we welcome you into the life of this community." The model of Benedictine hospitality outlined in the Rule provides us with a way to be Christ's welcoming servants today, both as receivers and givers of grace.

Benedictine Hospitality in the World

The British writer Esther de Waal, who has taught the way of Benedict out of her experience of living the Rule as a professor, mother, clergy spouse, and lay theologian, has perhaps done more than anyone to communicate the relevance of Benedictine spirituality to those outside the cloister today. In 1982 she offered the first Benedictine Experience in the precincts of Canterbury Cathedral, where a group lived for ten days following the rhythm of study, worship, and work outlined in the Rule.

Such offerings have continued in various parts of the world, as people who hunger for a balanced life in which prayer is central have discovered Benedict and his wisdom. Her book *Seeking God: The Way of Saint Benedict* offers practical insights into interpreting the Rule in the concrete situations and mundaneness of everyday life:

> There is a knock at the door and I have to respond; as I lay four extra places for supper I know that soon four people will

be sitting round the table sharing the meal. If I am actually afraid and defensive (or aggressive, which is much the same), anxious and insecure about the impression that I shall be making, I may offer a glass of sherry or a bowl of soup but any real hospitality of the heart will be lacking; I shall have merely fulfilled the social expectation. I cannot become a good host until I am at home in my own house, so rooted in my centre (as stability has taught) that I no longer need to impose my terms on others but can instead afford to offer them a welcome that gives them the chance to be completely themselves. Here again is the paradox, that by emptying myself I am not only able to give but also to receive.[8]

We can make our homes places of welcome where there is always room at the table for the friend our teenage daughter unexpectedly brings home, the grieving colleague who needs a respite from his now empty house, or the neighbor whose kitchen is being remodeled. Meals do not need to be elaborate; simple, wholesome food offered with grace as we accept the privilege of service feeds the souls as well as the bodies of our guests.

Our churches too can become spaces where we set a high priority on making the newcomer truly welcome. One large parish I know asked each member to provide his or her own ceramic mug for use during coffee hour to eradicate the need for nonrecyclable styrofoam cups. The congregation then provided blue coffee mugs for guests, alerting regular members of the church to notice and welcome "blue mug" newcomers. Another parish has established a group of greeters who each Sunday afternoon visit the homes of guests attending the morning service. The greeters carry with them a loaf of freshly baked bread and a card that says, "We are glad you worshiped with us today and hope you will break bread with us often. Welcome."

Recently some friends and I visited several Coptic monasteries located in the desert just south of Alexandria, Egypt. Here we met people who had chosen a life of prayer, discipline, silence, and simplicity lived in community. The monks occupied spartan cells, eating simple food with water at a premium. They worshiped in ancient chapels, some dating back to the fourth century C.E. To enter a chapel we removed our shoes, walked across carpeted floor, and gazed at icons—dozens of them beckoning worshipers to see divine presence beyond the image. The eyes drew me. The iconographers of past centuries conveyed purity, clarity, compassion, and a compelling interrogative in those eyes, eyes that welcomed and repelled, extended compassion and asked for integrity—that placed me in question.

The eyes of the monks also spoke most eloquently of love for God and generous hospitality. We were welcomed "as Christ," invited to be present in silence where centuries of Christian believers have prayed, and were given bread and wine so that we could celebrate our own Communion service in that holy space. Afterward they set a huge kettle of tea and home-baked, hearty bread before us.

The hospitality my friends and I received in the desert stands in sharp contrast to many vacuous social gatherings in which I participate. These monks gave out of their poverty and enriched me deeply by enabling me to see more clearly the compassionate Christ who longs to be living water in the dry places of my soul. They did not preach but participated in the joy of all creation, giving themselves fully that others might be filled. There was no posturing, no lavish spread to impress us, no empty conversation; but we left knowing ourselves accepted, fed, and called to give generously that others might be drawn to the heavenly banquet.

This is the kind of compassionate and joyous hospitality that Benedict extends in his Rule. Our eyes often speak more clearly than our words when strangers come among us and when we respond to those already in the circle whose actions hurt, irritate, or challenge us. We asked one of the Coptic monks how they know that a novice is ready to enter the community and take life vows. He replied, "We know by their eyes whether they are looking to God or looking to the world." Benedictine hospitality comes from correct vision, from seeing every person as a beloved child of God to be received without distinction: "Great care and concern are to be shown in receiving poor people and pilgrims, because in them more particularly Christ is received; our very awe of the rich guarantees them special respect."[9]

The school for the Lord's service offers remedial support as I struggle to let go of old ways of seeing and enter the discipline of refocusing my vision so that I recognize the Christ in all persons. I need to take off my shoes and enter the holy space where silence waits, where I am welcomed, and where I learn to extend the circle by smiling others into its inclusive center.

A Journal Entry

January 2, 1996

I am folded back into my space in front of the living room window as crows squawk, heater hums, and my body adjusts following a trans-Atlantic journey. As usual the "Welcome home" spoken by an immigration officer moved me. Rain falls; Bonnie, my cat, sleeps at my feet; and I name 1996 as the year of gentleness and so relax into this day without "pushing." I hear God's hospitable voice and know that I have all I need.

I just read the story of Elijah's resting after his fearful

flight from Jezebel and then eating the food provided while he slept, and it touches my need today. This is not high-energy time, and the creation of great spiritual goals to achieve would not be a gentle response to where I am. Instead I accept the tiredness, vulnerability, and need to be ministered to, and wait to eat from the divine fare that will be provided. And now I turn to the second scripture reading appointed today in *The Book of Common Prayer* lectionary and find it is the feeding of the 5,000 as recorded by John. Out of little Christ creates abundance and all are fed, whether or not they are worthy, understanding, grateful. This is grace. I am swimming in the ocean of God's abundance and know that today I will be fed with all that I need.

HOLY ONE, your welcome and gentle acceptance overwhelms me. I come gratefully to your table and pray for grace to be as Christ to others. May my words and my actions, my smile and my touch, show hospitality to all who come my way today. Amen.

SUGGESTIONS FOR REFLECTION

1. Scripture passage for *lectio divina*: Luke 7:36-50.

2. Take a walk with the awareness that you are a guest in this wonderful world that God has created. Notice the life-giving presence of beauty, growth, potential for blessing. Be aware too of the pollution and brokenness that invite action. Write a prayer that embodies your observations and response to God, who "speaks" through the created world.

3. As you consider Benedict's instruction, "Never give a hollow greeting of peace," ask yourself how you can really be present to others so that you see Christ in them. Who in the community needs your forgiveness? In what ways do you seek opportunities to bless by ministering to those in need, while remaining open to receive their gifts? Who needs your love in order to be gathered into the circle of your faith community?

THREE

SIMPLICITY

❀

*As we progress in this way of life
and in faith, we shall run on the path of God's
commandments, our hearts overflowing with
the inexpressible delight of love.*[1]

Great joy comes in embracing simplicity and becoming conscious of the rhythms that give shape to our lives. When I lived in New York, the city that never sleeps, I rarely saw the stars; and night sounds consisted of traffic, human voices, and the thuds of an antiquated heating system. It took time to adjust to the South Carolina Low Country, where cicadas, tree frogs, and other night creatures produced the only sounds in the Great Silence that followed Compline, the final prayers of the day. For the first time I became aware of the rhythm of light and darkness as residents of the Holy Savior Priory began worship in the predawn silence and entrusted each night to God when darkness fell. A bell summoned us to chapel five times a day; work, study, recreation, and meals together structured the day. This rhythm set us free, simplified our schedules, and brought balance to our lives.

Saint Benedict entered his cave in Subiaco seeking to make sense of his Christian commitment and to discern God's way in a torn-apart, troubled society. The fall of Rome and the rise of "barbarian" tribes, dissent in the church, and political disorder all contributed to the sense of chaos and meaninglessness. Benedict chose to simplify his life in order to be more available to God, to listen and to learn the way of Truth. Others with a similar yearning soon joined him, and guidelines for their life together became necessary; hence the Rule, for simplicity is not easy. There is risk involved in refusing to live by cultural norms, as well as struggle in trusting God for daily needs. Most of us will not be called to monastic life; our challenge is to find ways to let go intentionally of our dependency on things, status, and expectations. Only then can we make space for God's word. The principles of the Rule can help us as we seek a simpler lifestyle and as we apply Saint Benedict's wisdom to our personal rhythms and our attitudes toward food, work, sleep, recreation, worship, play, and discipline.

Consider the Lilies

A good place to begin this process of simplification is to reflect on the words of Jesus, spoken to those who were fearful about the future and doubtful of God's providence. Like so many of us they wanted security, predictable patterns of social and family life, certainty that things would not change in their worship communities. Lovingly Jesus confronts this faithless anxiety:

> Therefore I tell you, do not worry about your life, what you will eat or what you will drink, or about your body, what you will wear. Is not life more than food, and the body more than clothing? Look at the birds of the air; they neither sow nor reap nor gather into barns, and yet your heavenly Father feeds them. Are you not of more value than they? And can any of you by worrying add a single hour to your span of life? And

why do you worry about clothing? Consider the lilies of the field, how they grow; they neither toil nor spin, yet I tell you, even Solomon in all his glory was not clothed like one of these. But if God so clothes the grass of the field, which is alive today and tomorrow is thrown into the oven, will he not much more clothe you—you of little faith? Therefore do not worry, saying, "What will we eat?" or "What will we drink?" or "What will we wear?" For it is the Gentiles who strive for all these things; and indeed your heavenly Father knows that you need all these things. But strive first for the kingdom of God and his righteousness, and all these things will be given to you as well (Matt. 6:25-33).

Taking time out to observe the birds or watch the flowers grow puts us in touch with God's care and nature's rhythms. It reminds us that none of our insurance policies, investment accounts, or possessions can provide the safety we crave; and it throws us back on our Creator who asks us to risk everything so that our hearts overflow with "the inexpressible delight of love." God who calls us to risk is an inveterate risk-taker. The story of God's willingness to risk and trust goes back beyond time. God is not a tentative Creator who plays it safe by weaving predictability into the fabric of the universe. The account of creation offered in the first chapter of Genesis reveals a robust, playful act of divine faith by which God sets in motion a glorious evolution of matter and beings. A breathless sense of anticipation accompanies each phase, followed by a delighted exclamation—it is good! When all is done, and God's ultimate creative act has brought into being woman and man made together in the divine image, the work is celebrated as very good. Surely God's cause for gladness extends beyond the order of things to the wonderful possibility that now opens before the human pair to whom God entrusts the stewardship of the earth. The Creator invites them to become risk-takers, cocreators, caretakers in the intricate world of life and matter.

Our stewardship of the earth is one of responsibility and care rather than oppressive domination. The twelfth-century Benedictine mystic Hildegard of Bingen writes of the compassion that floods the entire universe. She teaches us that we are one with the cosmic Christ as our own compassionate loving touches all: "As human persons view creation with compassion in trust, they see the Lord. It is God which humankind is then able to recognize in every living thing."[2] Hildegard speaks of the web of the universe, the interconnectedness of every living thing, the Christ-presence in all that is. She paints a glorious picture of the unity of all things under Christ and offers an illumination, in mandala form, of cosmic harmony. Hildegard drew her inspiration from her environment, which spoke to her of God's loving nurture of things.

Today the sisters at the Abbey of Saint Hildegard continue to work in the fields, producing some of the finest wine on the Rhine from the grapes that grow abundantly in orderly rows. Like Saint Benedict's monks, the sisters have some outside help, but they regard the manual labor involved in producing crops as a prayer offering, an opportunity to celebrate creation.

The ordering of creation has for too long been predominantly interpreted as separation among its many elements and a domination by the greatest over that which has less value. Such thinking is not implied in the original account of Creation, nor is it the only thread of interpretation running through history. The Genesis narrative implies connectedness and invites respect for every particle of matter and every creature.

In order to love the earth we need to know it for what it is, which may require a radical shift in our thinking. We have become accustomed to regarding earth's resources as primarily there for us to use, as though they had no intrinsic worth beyond their value to us. We have harnessed water and mass produced harvests. Factory farming has grown as our demand for inexpensive and ready-prepared food products has increased. Our demand for fast, prepackaged food has resulted in a stripping of rain forests—essential to the natural balance of the environment—in order to provide pasture land for more cattle so that our hamburgers will cost less. In the process, many indigenous peoples have been rendered homeless, and the habitat of endangered species has been lost forever. Much of the food sold by fast food chains is packaged in styrofoam containers, which constitute a hazard to the environment: They are not biodegradable and produce poisonous gases if burned.

Goods come to us from unknown manufacturers, food from distant places, fuel from underground conduits. We have demanded efficiency, speed, and convenience as our lifestyles have become more complex. Most of us have little direct involvement with the living, growing things so necessary to sustain life. It is not surprising that we often lack a sense of connectedness to and stewardship for the earth since we do not touch, nourish, or see it. Increasingly this alienation has caused us to forget our place in the total scheme of things. The cry of Henry David Thoreau, "Simplify, simplify...," calls us to a spirituality rooted in simplicity. His choice, more than a century ago, to reside in a rustic shelter and live as simply as possible on what he could grow or earn by his labor led him to rich insights about the nature of humanity and what we really need.[3] Saint Benedict had pointed the way to this kind of simplicity fourteen centuries earlier.

Our alienation from the earth perhaps reflects a cultural obsession even deeper than convenience. It may be that the vast amount of energy our culture expends on speed and efficiency represents an attempt to eliminate or minimize risk. We want predictability; and where life is uncertain, we are ready to pay in order to avoid the discomfort of living with its vicissitudes. In the process we can easily lose sight of the transforming newness that takes place each time we act like our Creator, trusting ourselves to what is unknown and different.

Simplicity as a Countercultural Choice

Our movement toward simplicity, toward a more Godlike embracing of life, is therefore countercultural. It challenges the assumption that human well-being requires predictability. It causes us to question cultural norms that demand convenient, instant, or synthetic commodities at the expense of whole peoples and ecosystems. More than that, it brings into focus a lost image of power, not the supposed power of acquisitiveness and domination but, the divine energy of imagination set free to re-vision the cosmos. This hopeful, active imagination invites us to live and work in such a way that God can continue to see a "very good" world.

It is no longer enough to discuss ecology across the coffee table or to theorize about how much time we have before water supplies become so polluted or the ozone layer so reduced that human life is threatened. Now is the moment for commitment, for staking life on making God's presence known in rock, ocean, and forest. Now is the moment to resist relentlessly every act of violence against creation. Some of us will be drawn to public and prophetic action that calls attention in dramatic ways to the devastating future we face if we refuse to change. Others will be drawn to less noticeable forms of action. Our prayer needs to be one of discernment: How does God want me to act, choose, pray in this moment so that my way of life enhances the goodness of creation?

How do we begin to know this earth and so regain that reverence for life that leads to change? The first step in this process is to recognize that we are an integral part of all that is, not superior beings for whom everything else is there to be used. We are woven into the "web of the universe," and nothing we do is without significance to the rest. We will then need to wrestle prayerfully with questions about how we can adopt a simpler lifestyle, even if simplifying means letting go of some of the quick and easy ways of living on which we have learned to depend. A simpler lifestyle will mean opting for less convenient but more wholesome things. Few of us will feel called to the spartan simplicity of Saint Benedict or Thoreau (whose experiment living in the woods by Walden Pond was only a brief interlude in his life), but we will be invited to examine our attitude to things. Our question may be, "How do I share the many resources available to me and cease to be dominated by the obsession for more?"

Beyond the personal inconvenience of simplifying our lives lies an even more disconcerting issue. The destructive aspects of our affluent lifestyle often seem so vast that a hopeless inertia may tempt us to give up. I stop eating hamburgers from a particular fast food chain or insist on organically grown vegetables or carry my own reusable bag when I go to the grocery store. So what? Does this really have any lasting impact on the global problems of our day? Behind these questions lies the assumption that only what is large and observable has value. When we begin to live a spirituality of simplicity, our primary concern ceases to be success and becomes faithfulness. We are called to live with integrity, to express the truth as we perceive it, and to trust in God's ability to use what we offer.

Certainly we will want our attempts to reverse the destructive patterns of life in the world to result in change (although the motivation for that change may be somewhat different from that of the majority, who now realize that we must act to save the planet). At the heart of our prayer and action rests the conviction that this is God's world and any misuse of its resources dishonors the Creator. As stewards of all that is good we know ourselves to be called to act responsibly: beyond the urgent need to save the earth for human benefit to the even more powerful motive of glorifying the One who made us.

Listening to the Voice of Nature

A starting point for hearing God's invitation to action is learning to listen with the ears of our heart as Benedict instructs. Words from the media, colleagues, and our mailboxes bombard us; an endless number of billboards assaults us along our highways. Sometimes we pay attention to what is spoken from the pulpit, but often our worship services are so busy and full of words that they have little effect. We need to give some time simply to being in the presence of the created universe with no other purpose than to attend to what is there. Listening to the voice of nature will help us attune ourselves to the words of God spoken in silence to the deep places of our being:

> The heavens declare the glory of God,
>   and the firmament shows his handiwork.
> One day tells its tale to another,
>   and one night imparts knowledge to another.
> Although they have no words or language,
>   and their voices are not heard,
> Their sound has gone out into all lands,
>   and their message to the ends of the earth.
>   —Psalm 19:1-4, BCP

Such deep listening can lead to the wonder expressed by the psalmist:

> When I consider your heavens, the work of your fingers,
> The moon and the stars you have set on their courses,
> What [are mortals] that you should be mindful of [them]?
> —Psalm 8:3-4, BCP

The psalmist sees himself not as the center of the universe but as a small yet profoundly privileged person within it. The rest of the psalm is an act of worship praising God the Creator and exalting the name of the Holy One.

We cannot always be in a place where the sun rises from the ocean or gentle streams speak of tranquility and renew our spirit. But the unattainable does not cut us off from presence to created things. Most of us have access to a collection of objects from nature—stones, feathers, pine cones, a flower, or blade of grass. Spending fifteen minutes simply being with an object, noticing its texture and color, and allowing it to "speak" of its origin or to generate thought of God's creative love may be as fruitful a meditation as long hours of Bible study. In fact, the object may well call forth biblical images and ideas that lead us deeper into prayer as we realize our connection with the earth.

The present ecological crisis provides an opportunity to experience afresh some of the joys of simplicity lost to us through the frenetic activity of affluence. Our "instant" way of life has deeply affected families. From the credit card to instant cleaning products and headache cures, we have come to expect no-wait commodities and have fallen into a no-time attitude toward one another. What if we planned at least one family meal together each week—a celebration that each member of the household helped prepare—instead of each person fixing his or her own rapid meal before rushing off to the next activity? The sacramental nature of eating together might be rediscovered in this simple event. Such a rediscovery could lead us into recognition of the holiness deep within us all that reminds us who we are in relation to our Creator.

The attentiveness that allows us to be present to nature and to each other awakens in us a sense of wonder. Here small children have much to teach us. Children, blessed with a natural sense of wonder, often become absorbed for long periods of time in the presence of natural things. Sand, water, rocks, and woodlands provide magical playgrounds and offer great scope for the imagination. Sadly much of our formal as well as informal education encourages us to move from contemplative wonder into the world of rational thought and technological competence where we find no place to dream. A spirituality of simplicity will affirm children in their attention to creation. But it will also recognize the child in each of us who wants to observe, play, and live fully in the marvelous world of God's making. We will reflect the robust playfulness of God (who made Leviathan "for the sport of it" [Ps. 104:27, BCP]) in our own surprised delight as we learn to touch, taste, and see the miracle of creativity.

Planting things, waiting for them to mature, and caring for them through the seasons of growth are a wonderful way to be in touch with and pray our love for creation. The smallest yard provides some space for plants. Nurseries now sell apple trees that will grow in a pot and produce fruit directly from the stem! Even in an apartment a small herb garden is possible. There is so much joy to celebrate when the long time of waiting yields its fruit, and we can enjoy the produce of our labor. We can easily obtain out-of-season produce, so we have lost the excitement that comes from the first taste of long-awaited fruit. As a child I delighted in the first plump raspberry picked from the bush and the field mushrooms we gathered in early fall. They seemed to burst with flavor in a way that those in the plastic-covered packages do not. Might not a spirituality of simplicity cause us to consider ways in which we regain a sense of ourselves as gardeners and growers?

Discovering the artist within ourselves is also a natural response to being immersed in love for creation and the Creator. Created in God's image, we are creators. Much of the world's poetry has been born in the context of wonder at the marvels of nature. "The world is charged with the grandeur of God,"[4] wrote Gerard Manley Hopkins, who found his pen overflowing with praise as he contemplated creation. He expressed his stewardship through the beauty of writing; others have done so through painting, making pottery, carving, weaving, spinning, or building.

The desire for simplicity leads some of us to value skills nearly lost and to search out natural expressions of creativity. When the rediscovery of these skills emerges not only from a wistful or nostalgic longing for the past but also from a yearning to express the divine within ourselves, then we learn to live more simply and to pray in a more integrated fashion. Our creativity will become our prayer, born of simple attention to what is around us. We enhance the world through its expression.

Simplicity was as much a keynote in Jesus' teaching as it was in his choice of lifestyle. He constantly referred to things in creation to illustrate his point.

> When you are discouraged at the apparent slowness with which people embrace the good news, remember what happens when you put yeast into dough. It grows and keeps on growing, not always perceptibly but steadily, so have patience. Above all, learn to pay attention, listen, observe, take time to process what you receive. When a farmer scatters seed, it falls

in a variety of places and produces healthy grain only when it is received into well-prepared soil. Allow yourself the time to sense what is right so that you may discern God's presence and respond to it (Matt. 6:25-33, AP).

Our courage to be agents of change in the world finds its source in the life and teaching of Jesus, who gives us the power to call ourselves children of God (John 1:12). As members of the divine family, a loving Creator offers all the resources that empower us to live with joy, playfulness, and risk as we care for the earth. When Jesus entered the Temple precincts and found them contaminated by commerce, exploitation, and greed, he acted swiftly and decisively. He drove the merchants out, spoiled their goods, and cast their coinage to the ground. The wind of zeal for the holiness of God blew through that place, revealing the hollow motivations of those with merchandise to offer.

Today the environment offers a parallel place of pollution as we see it diminished by commercial greed and by the suspicion that makes us stockpile nuclear weapons to destroy each other. In this holy place we stand as stewards of a loving and holy God, and we give ourselves to the task of restoration as we embrace a deeper simplicity.

Today no bells call me to stop what I am doing and join others in prayer, so I need to find ways to create appropriate rhythms as I try to simplify my life. I am wakened by the alarm clock's buzzing, an invitation to the first prayer of the day, a brief committing of time to God. Following my shower I sit with coffee for a time of reflection asking God for the grace to be present to the divine word in scripture and later through the people and events of the day. I read the biblical lessons using the well-tried model of *lectio divina* that has sustained Benedictines for many centuries; prayer follows from the reading.

Usually I record insights, desires, needs in my journal. This early morning time has become the bedrock on which I ground my day. In the evening I choose to spend time recalling the day: blessings received, opportunities missed, grace given in difficult situations, joyous surprises. All become the stuff of prayer calling forth gratitude, repentance, intercession, adoration, and specific requests for what I need from God tomorrow. The brief night office of Compline ends this time of letting go.

These two intentional prayer times give shape to the day and, together with a period of walking meditation, form a structure to help me continue listening to the word through work, conversations, and events. I learned recently that John Wesley dedicated five minutes of every waking hour to prayer, which has challenged me to look for ways of incorporating brief prayer times at other points in the day. At the moment that seems to work best as I become conscious of transition times—ending a phone conversation, leaving the office, going into a meeting. I now silently offer a prayer before moving on.

The process of simplification continues, and it is hard. I read Saint Benedict's instructions regarding the right amount of food and drink and feel embarrassed by the indigestion medicine in the bathroom cabinet. I hear Benedict give instruction about simple clothing and reluctantly pass the mall entrance or put down the mail-order catalogue. The instructions about caring for and reusing tools challenge me when I am tempted to buy foil throwaway containers or toss unwanted mail into the trash instead of recycling it. My valuing of creation as Benedict did draws me outside to tend my yard or hike in the mountains instead of opting for some mindless escape that leaves my soul empty and my body inert. Saint Benedict also reminds me that recreation is essential—a lesson I need to have reinforced daily as a child of this driven, workaholic culture.

A Journal Entry

December 1989

Last night
sun-fall
turned the sea's edge
into a muted rainbow.
Soft peach and turquoise
moving to deepest indigo.
A big flock of gulls
crowded the shore.
The child within me
stirred.
I ran, arms flailing,
among them,
and watched their wild scattering.
With my passing they returned,
resting by pools
to wait the night.

ETERNAL ONE, revealed in waves and in the waiting stillness, teach me to rest, content in your love. Let my life be a poem that tells of your care, always ready to rise up on trusting wings and risk the wind. Amen.

SUGGESTIONS FOR REFLECTION

1. Scripture passage for *lectio divina*: Luke 10:3-9.

2. Take some time to reflect on the events, committees, and programs that claim your time and on the magazines, mail-order catalogues, and papers you read. Which of these might you relin-

quish in order to simplify your life? What other time-consuming activities become unnecessary as you claim more space for listening to God's invitation to simplicity?

3. Carry a small rock in a pocket to remind you often of your desire to "simplify, simplify."

FOUR

PRAYER

*The oratory ought to be what it is called,
and nothing else is to be done or stored there.
After the Work of God, all should leave in complete
silence and with reverence for God, so that a
brother who may wish to pray alone will not be
disturbed by the insensitivity of another.
Moreover, if at other times someone chooses to pray
privately, he may simply go in and pray, not in a
loud voice, but with tears and heartfelt devotion.
Accordingly, anyone who does not pray in this
manner is not to remain in the oratory after the
Work of God, as we have said; then he will
not interfere with anyone else.[1]*

Prayer is work. Saying prayers alone and participating in
corporate worship make up one small part of what prayer is all
about, and these two aspects sometimes can shield us from the
awesome task of growing into God. We are beloved children
of a loving Creator who, through Christ, invites us into ever
deepening intimacy, an intimacy we sometimes welcome but
often fear. Prayer is the context in which we confront our fears,

73

recognize resistance, let go of demands for immediate solutions to life's dilemmas, and learn to wait. The work of prayer consists of ceasing from chatter and learning to listen, relinquishing our supposed control of the situation and letting God be God. This is hard work.

Prayer also seems like hard work at those times when we lack a sense of God's presence so that it becomes a duty and not a joy. Then it may be time to examine the image of God that we carry. Unless we can be at home with God no matter what emotional turmoil may envelop us, then we will certainly not be inclined to enter a conversation with God. The best we may be able to do is try to talk above the discomfort of our feelings, pretending that all is well and failing to hear the word that can free us. We do not have to begin the conversation; instead we are invited to listen, simply to be in God's presence with all our questions, confusion, and anxiety, knowing that nothing can separate us from the love of God. When we understand this we can begin to respond, bringing to the dialogue all that once seemed to distance us from the One to whom we pray.

In chapter 4 of the Rule, Saint Benedict offers us "The Tools for Good Works." His first instruction is, "Love the Lord God with your whole heart." Here he quotes the gospel demand to give God the first place in our affections. Later in the chapter he says, "Listen readily to holy reading, and devote yourself often to prayer." He ends the chapter with encouragement to "never lose hope in God's mercy." [2] As we strive to give God first place in our lives, we become aware of self-interest and of the conflict between God's way and our desires. Only through listening again and again to scripture, immersing ourselves in prayer, and trusting in God's inexhaustible mercy may we consent to the ever-deepening relationship into which God calls us.

Because Benedict lived in a pre-Freudian world, he does not speak in familiar psychological terms. However, applying some contemporary insights into the human psyche may help us as we learn to understand ourselves and our fear of intimacy with God. It may be that the images of God that we unconsciously carry into prayer actually prevent us from relating deeply because they reflect our projections of human experience with our primary childhood caregivers.

Our "work" may begin with the willingness to examine some of our presuppositions about who God is for us. I found this to be true for me when I spent time reflecting on my own parents, who raised me in the best way they could. My British father was caring but "distant"; I can remember no close physical contact, no hugs or embraces. He did not beat me, but I somehow grew up feeling that I did not measure up, was not good enough to deserve his affirmation. I tried very hard to make him notice and appreciate me, tried to be his perfect little girl, but I received sparse reward for all my effort. When I thought about these aspects as an adult, I realized that this experience conditioned my image of God as Father. I could talk about grace and unconditional love, but I did not live it. Instead I saw myself primarily in terms of failing to measure up to God's demands: unworthy, imperfect, and undeserving of acceptance.

This distorted image of God did not encourage intimacy. I prayed because I *should* do so, trying to win approval by praying better and longer with great earnestness. Over time I have learned to become an iconoclast, to smash those images that rob me of God's compassion. As the father-projection became evident, I recalled the no-nonsense, absolute acceptance of my maternal grandmother whose home was a magical refuge full of delights, with many hiding places where imagination could take flight. A dress-up box of discarded clothes—veils, hats, high-heeled shoes—and a large cookie tin full of treasures became the source of endless, joyful play. I began to find in this memory some divine characteristics previously absent from consciousness when I prayed. In my grandmother's eyes I felt loved whether my behavior was good or bad. Disobedience brought consequences but not rejection, and being with her was joyous. I felt welcomed, safe, set free to explore the wonderful world of creative imagination. Now I began to see God in broader terms, no longer only as Judge but as compassionate, generous, welcoming Creator with whom I celebrated playfulness and the gift of creativity.

Praying the Psalms

For many centuries the recitation of the Psalter has provided the primary rhythm of prayer for monastic communities. The psalmist's statement, "Seven times a day do I praise you" (Ps. 119:164, BCP), gave rise to the sevenfold Daily Office, now often reduced to four, in which the psalms were chanted. Saint Benedict urges his community, "Let us stand to sing the psalms in such a way that our minds are in harmony with our voices."[3] To that end the monks took great care to prepare adequately for singing the Divine Office. Monastic chant enjoys great popularity today, even in the secular world, but it is hard work! I well remember my first weeks in the monastery trying to learn the pointing of the psalms, the many tones, and the variety of antiphons that began and ended our singing of the Psalter. It seemed I would never become proficient, and weekly choir practice was a difficult and often tedious activity. Many months passed before I realized the importance of this constant practice. Singing the psalms each day involved *work*, requiring familiarity with the chants and conscious effort to bring my mind in harmony with my voice as I sang.

The psalms continue to be an integral part of my prayer and the means through which I try to listen to the word. They express the full range of human emotion, excluding God from none of it. They open up a way to pray authentically, to engage in the work of prayer that refuses to take refuge in a domesticated God who smooths life's rough edges. These old prayers and songs are vibrantly alive, new, and inviting. In them we hear the expression of joy, hope, lament, rage, fear, oppression, trust, and abandonment that is part of our experience too. There are moments of triumph in which God is blessed, and there are times of tragedy when life is emptied of meaning and God seems absent.All the extremes of human experience find a place in the prayer of the Psalter.

Our desire for equilibrium can become an idolatrous attempt to deny a large part of what life is about. The advertising industry achieves much of its success through the message that this or that product will satisfy our needs and longings. We can fix our not-yet-perfect lives by obtaining the right house, floor polish, insurance policy, or therapy. In other words, advertising media encourages us to believe that something is wrong with us if our lives are out of kilter, if we don't live on a plateau of happiness. The psalms give the lie to this kind of thinking by supporting our efforts to deal robustly with life as it really is and to find God in disorientation as well as harmony. It comes as both a relief and a challenge to comprehend that there is no place where God is not.

Psalm 139 speaks of the attempt to escape the Creator by soaring into the heavens, going into the depths, or sinking into the horizon where sea and sky meet. The sense of God's being behind, in front, and above, laying a hand upon the one who feels searched out and known, makes the omnipresence of the Creator a felt reality. I pray this psalm and have to ask, "Who am I? How can I respond to this all-encompassing presence of God?" In my time and place I am on holy ground and as I allow myself to be held in that moment of awareness, I must respond with what is in my heart. I tell God about my fear, my relief, my gratitude, or my overwhelming sense of being invaded.

The seasons of our life will condition our response to the God who encounters us in the psalms. Again Psalm 139 offers a good example. When I feel that I am in a precarious place, I experience relief to know that God surrounds me. When I am caught up in prideful ambition, I may wish to place distance between us. The psalm raises my awareness of my personal experience at that prideful moment and, in the process, puts me in touch with the Source of my life. It offers no magic "fix" but sets me to the task of figuring out the most appropriate response to the One who loved me into being. Often that response will invite change!

Thanksgiving and celebration play a central role in the life of God's people. Many psalms commemorated great redeeming acts and times of triumph or victory over enemies. Dancing, music, and festive joy filled the community as the Israelites rejoiced together, praising the God of their deliverance. Our own joy resonates with theirs as we recall the giftedness of our lives and the times God has saved us from the enemies of despair, fear, and pain. Sometimes the reading of psalms such as 145–150 reminds me of the many reasons I have to offer thanks to God— a reminder I often need when wants and longings seem unfulfilled. Without opting for a Pollyanna style of happiness that denies the troubled aspects of life, I can allow God to call gratitude out of me for all that is good in my experience.

Praise the Lord, O my soul!
  I will praise the Lord as long as I live;
I will sing praises to my God while I have my being.
                                    —Psalm 146:1-2, BCP

Many Christians have difficulty with the psalms of revenge or curse and would banish them from the Psalter. However, this banishing effectively denies a real part of our experience. While we are to forgive our enemies and pray for those who hurt us, we usually can arrive at that place of forgiveness only when we acknowledge the vindictive rage we bear toward them. In expressing our desire for revenge, we tell God who we are—hurting, broken people not yet able to relinquish our pain—and we give the rage to God. Often in the psalms we see a healing taking place and a fresh vision of reality emerging as the psalmist pours out all the bitterness and disappointment. Psalm 55 exemplifies this expression of righteous indignation (and some paranoia) that leads to healing and hope:

> I am shaken by the noise of the enemy
>   and by the pressure of the wicked;
> ....
> We took sweet counsel together,
>   and walked with the throng in the house of God.
> Let death come upon them suddenly;
> let them go down alive into the grave;
>   for wickedness is in their dwellings, in their very midst.
>   —Psalm 55:2-3, 15-16, BCP

When I feel betrayed and oppressed, I need to share with God my longing for vengeance. When I choose to bury it instead, I increase the likelihood of its erupting inappropriately in a far more destructive form.

The seasons of lament also find a place in the Psalter. At

times life is sad. When disaster, sickness, and loss overwhelm us, we need to express our anguish to God. The best known of the corporate psalms of lament is 137, where members of the covenant community languishing in Babylon cry out their hopelessness: "How shall we sing the Lord's song upon an alien soil?" (v. 4, BCP). Exile has robbed them of the Temple and all other familiar structures that offered security. Wailing and mourning are fitting responses to the painful experience of loss; they appropriately give God their tears. Here too the psalms can give voice to our own experiences of anguish. The parent with Alzheimer's disease, the friend with AIDS, the death of one we love cause us to cry out in our impotence, bewailing the losses of life. The Compassionate One hears and weeps with us and in due time enables us to find redemption even in the void.

Many of the psalms reflect the pilgrim nature of the community. Sometimes these celebrate the gathering in Jerusalem for great festivals and the reenactment of God's interventions in human history that sustain the pilgrims in their present uncertainties. Many psalms also convey the individual sense of traveling, sometimes securely but often hesitantly, on a precarious journey. The valley of the shadow of death is as much a part of the experience as the green pastures and still waters (Psalm 23), for persons in pilgrimage are not static. Our own journey has many contours and leads us through places where specters of fear threaten our willingness to continue. The psalms help us to go on, to identify with those who have run and stumbled before us, and to find, as they did, the unseen presence of God in all our wandering.

Feelings of dereliction and abandonment are also a reality for those who commit themselves to follow honestly the Creator God who takes risks again and again. The Word that spoke the universe into being was God's affirmation of risk, and the Word that became flesh embodied risk and knew all our human frailty. When Christ cried out his sense of abandonment using the words of Psalm 22, he expressed the agonizing experience of an absent God and of a risk that seemed not to have paid off. There are seasons of life when the isolation and abandonment are so great that nothing less than the screaming of our "Why?" to God can be true prayer. Rationalizing, blaming, and explaining become hollow attempts to vindicate God by the denial of our experience, and we fall into the category of Job's "comforters" with their banal platitudes. The death of six million Jews, Mahatma Gandhi, Oscar Romero, or Martin Luther King Jr., as well as the pointless deaths of those we know more intimately, demand that we pray our feelings of God's absence.

Many of the psalms were written for liturgical use and to celebrate God's presence among the people, especially in the Temple. The enthronement of the Davidic king and his representative position as God's vice-regent gave cause for great thanksgiving. Psalm 110 expresses the victory of the earthly king who owes his position and success to God whom he serves. God's epiphany happens as humans enact their history in the place of worship; the liturgy reveals the presence of the holy God among a holy people. And so it is still. In both Jewish and Christian worship the Psalter serves as a vehicle that manifests the divine presence. In our personal reading of the psalms God comes to us also.

During my five years at the monastery the psalms became very familiar because we sang them day in and day out. The psalms sometimes reminded me of waves washing on the beach, for they formed a rhythm out of which we expressed our life. Our singing of the psalms moved beyond simple cognitive recitation of ancient words to being an experience of immersion in the psalms' acknowledgment of God's reality in all the vicissitudes of life. I felt drawn into their rhythmic flow of sound and into connectedness with all the millions of God's people who have prayed through them across the ages.

Matins took place at 5:30 AM. I did not always feel connected, glad to be called by the bell to worship, or awake at that time in the morning! Yet somehow, as the Psalter began, I found myself caught up again into the pattern of ancient worship, and the psalms prayed for me. A commitment to this kind of recitation of the offices has the advantage of removing prayer from the realm of my moods. So whether I feel like it or not, I say or sing the psalms because they help me develop my relationship with God. Sometimes I am bored, sometimes distressed, and sometimes inexplicably thrilled by the words as they become mine and take on fresh meaning. I am beyond the honeymoon phase of relationship and must now live the everydayness of life together, allowing God to have more and more space in my life as I grow in intimacy.

Praying Where We Are

Of course, it is not necessary to live in a monastic community in order to incorporate the psalms into daily worship. When I served a parish in New York City, the psalms sustained me. Sitting in my tiny studio apartment with the sound of garbage trucks and sirens far down in the street below, I found that the Psalter provided a beginning to my day: a far cry maybe from the Temple in Jerusalem but a necessary link with the Hebrew Scriptures to which I owe so much and to those unknown prayers in vastly different times and contexts who have allowed psalm prayer to enrich them. Often a phrase or thought, maybe a fresh image of God, would emerge as I read the words, and that would go with me into the day, inserting itself periodically into my frenetic schedule. Speaking the words aloud helped both with awareness of meaning and with attentiveness. Journaling with whatever emerged from my reading also served to reinforce what the psalm said to me and often led to further reflection upon it. It continues to fulfill that purpose as I now pray the psalms each morning in the mountains of North Carolina.

As we allow the psalms to provide rhythm for our lives and as we use them to express the various seasons of our experience, they may stimulate our own creativity. We can begin to write our own psalms! To employ a simple method, choose an existing psalm as a model and change some of the images so that you celebrate your own observation of God's presence in the midst of life. Using verses from Psalm 104, Maxwell Corydon Wheat Jr. moves the locus of the psalm from the hills and valleys of Judea to the Long Island salt marsh:

PSALM OF THE SALT MARSH
O Lord, my God, you are the Creator
You make the tides rise
    into the marsh grasses
bringing sustenance to every
    quahog in the creeks
To every blue mussel on the banks
To every egret stalking
    yellow tiptoe by yellow tiptoe
    plunging its long bill for mummichug
    The salt marsh is flooded with your ecology.[4]

The psalms, while old, remain ever new. I return again and again to the same words, but each time I come from a fresh time and place. T. S. Eliot speaks of our arriving at the same place in our journey and knowing it for the first time. That is often the sense I have with the psalms; I have stood on this rock, been in this pit, known this joy in the company of God's people. It is the same and yet it is not the same, for I still travel and still see in new ways as God nudges and sometimes drives me along on my human pilgrimage.

A Journal Entry

March 29, 1996

I come to my journal at this time with a sense of hard work lying before me in order to recover awareness and a sense of intimacy with God. Grace reminds me to let go. Spring birds caught my attention as I opened the door for Bonnie and now they continue their persistent sound— new songs. So here I am at the end of a long, over-busy time, sitting not with blame but with gratitude for today. A dream image comes to mind: As I get into my car the emergency brake comes away in my hand and I mutter, "Give me a break!" I love dream humor, which sometimes conveys truth in a more palatable way than rational thought. God is inviting me to let go of the busy activities that seem so essential and simply to rest in this time.

Loving Companion, hold me in your compassionate silence. Let me see clearly the barriers I have erected to keep you at a distance, so that my walk with you today may deepen my desire to listen and to love you always. Amen.

1. Scripture passage for *lectio divina*: Isaiah 43:1-4a.

2. The following exercise, based on the assumption that we have entered into an agreement with God that is usually unconscious and unexplored, can help us identify our current images of God and their source.

    a) Begin by recalling early memories of parenting and authority figures. What "messages" did you receive?

    b) Ask yourself, "How have these memories and messages affected my prayer?" For example, do I relate to God as a domineering parent, an absent caregiver, a rewarder of good behavior, overdemanding, forgetful of promises, too busy to pay attention to me?

    c) Consider the behavior patterns that have developed from your history. What "shoulds," "musts," "oughts" that were imposed on you do you now impose on yourself? How do these condition the agreement?

    d) Write a sentence based on this old agreement beginning, "I am your person as long as..." For example, "I am good enough," "you do what I ask," etc.

    e) Think about how this perception has conditioned your relationship with God, and identify ways in which you need to change or replace the image. Tell God of your desire to grow in intimacy and of any resistance this generates.

3. Write your own psalm. If you choose, take one of the biblical psalms as a pattern for your own observations and desires.

FIVE

MANUAL LABOR

❀

*Idleness is the enemy of the soul. Therefore, the
brothers should have specified periods for manual
labor as well as for prayerful reading.*[1]

EACH YEAR the farmer who harvested fields around the South
Carolina monastery presented the community with a large sack
of grain. During the fall, monks and guests were put to work
laboriously sifting wheat and removing the chaff by hand as it
surfaced. Then the grain was tipped into an ancient and very
noisy mill that produced a coarse, fresh whole wheat flour used
to bake bread twice weekly. These firm and wholesome loaves
received wide acclaim, and often visitors told us they had never
tasted anything so good. The same flour was used to produce
the flat eucharistic bread that was broken and shared daily.

This labor intensive activity of grinding flour and knead-
ing bread dough was one of the most popular work assignments for retreatants who chose to participate in the whole
Benedictine rhythm of the monastery. I think I understand
why as I remember my own first visit there during the years I

lived in Manhattan. Flying to Charleston, South Carolina, climbing down the steps from the plane—no jetways at the airport in 1983!—breathing the warm, pungent air, and driving through rural Low Country landscape intensified my expectations that this retreat would mark a transition point. We turned off the highway, and the Prior brought me up the mile-long, unpaved road edged by wheat, corn, and cotton fields and installed me in my "hermitage." I rested, prayed, walked, and worshiped with the monks in their new chapel, where large windows revealed ancient oaks festooned with Spanish moss and turtles laying eggs in the sandy soil. And I made flour.

Alone in the barn I sifted the wheat and began to think of John the Baptist's preaching about the One who was to come with winnowing fork in hand to separate wheat from chaff. "Repent" cried the forerunner of Christ, and I seemed to hear an invitation to consider where God was calling me to conversion. The work continued, and the words of Jesus now addressed me: "Unless a grain of wheat falls into the earth and dies, it remains just a single grain; but if it dies, it bears much fruit" (John 12:24).

This verse spoke to me of letting go, of being willing to remain in darkness, the darkness of not knowing and ambiguity, until the time came to push up toward the light. Gestation was the message and I was asked simply to be, without forcing growth or demanding immediate results. I offered the time of retreat into God's hands, praying for the grace to receive whatever the days might bring instead of demanding rewarding experiences in prayer. This openness required conversion and a willingness to deal with impatience.

More sifting. The work now became tedious, and I wanted to reach the next stage of actually grinding the grain so that I could see the end product—fresh, mealy flour. I was tempted to take short cuts, to miss a few pieces of chaff, and I realized that I had already shifted from the attentiveness that enabled me to be present to this work in this moment. I wanted to return and let go of impatience. So I allowed the centuries-old Jesus Prayer to help me refocus, "Lord, Jesus Christ, have mercy on me." In this prayer repeated over and over again, I acknowledged that Jesus is Lord, and I acknowledged dependence on Christ's merciful compassion. I returned to the now, sifting, casting out the chaff, discarding my desire to be done with activity as I allowed it to claim my effort.

Finally I ground the sifted grains and began to scoop the flour into ziplock bags, storing some in the freezer and taking others to the kitchen where the flour would be made into the next batch of bread. Then the cleanup! Again I had to deal with the inclination to "get it over with" and thereby withdraw my caring attention from this task. Unless I cleaned the mill carefully and removed all residue of flour, it would quickly become home to weevils. The next user would have to spend much time disposing of them before work could begin again. That fact made me aware of others' involvement in the labor of the monastery. I realized that the way I did my work would reveal my respect for and cooperation with them. So I thoroughly cleaned the mill.

Now I heard the bell summon us to noonday prayer—three hours gone. As I walked to the chapel, I carried images of the stubblefields I had passed on my way to the monastery, the brown grains I had separated from the chaff, the white flour dropping down the chute from the millstones, and the wonderful grainy bread I had enjoyed at breakfast. I had participated in a process of which I was usually unaware, and I felt a deep connectedness with creation and with those who share this planet with me. Someone had plowed the fields and sowed the seed. The sun and rain had caused the once hidden grain to grow. Others had fertilized, then harvested the wheat before presenting it to the monastery, where one of the monks had made the bread that nourished us. What the Creator began we had, together, continued.

For a number of reasons this work activity was deeply rewarding to me and many other retreatants, not least of which was the way it enabled us to reconnect with creation. For most of us the work also represented a change in pace; it slowed us down and gave us time to reflect while engaged in simple, manual tasks. As we worked we began to recognize that what we did would directly touch the lives of others, that we were part of a wider community. Manual labor gradually became prayer as we undertook the task with care and attention and as the activity itself generated images that called us to listen and dialogue with Christ the Word.

Saint Benedict gave great value to such work, building periods of it into the daily schedule. In his rural environment caring for crops was part of the monks' livelihood, though others may have done some of the actual work. However, he instructs, "They must not become distressed if local conditions or their poverty should force them to do the harvesting themselves. When they live by the labor of their hands, as our fathers and the apostles did, then they are really monks."[2] His reference to the apostles no doubt alludes to Paul's statement about working with his own hands to support himself and companions (Acts 20:34) and to his letter to the Thessalonian Christians in which he castigates them for living in idleness as mere busybodies (2 Thess. 3:11). Benedict wants all of his monks to engage in work; even the sick or weak are to be given some task or craft that will keep them busy.

The Rule deals with work assignments in the kitchen, dining hall, library, chapel, guest quarters, and fields. The monastery had no slaves, modeled not on the secular world but on the servant ministry to which Jesus called his disciples (John 13). Tasks were rotated, and monks undertook the work in a spirit of humility for the well-being of the whole community. All goods and tools of the monastery were entrusted to a monk in whose manner of life the abbot had confidence, and Benedict says, "Whoever fails to keep the things belonging to the monastery clean or treats them carelessly should be reproved."[3] This was not a throw-away community but one in which one gave the same attentiveness and care to work tools as to sacred vessels and books. The monks learned that prayer is work and work is prayer. If any were in the fields when the bell rang and too far from the oratory to arrive on time, they were to perform the work of God where they were. Prayer is doing with reverence and attention whatever is required of one at a given moment.

Prayer as Conscious Living

The Rule of Saint Benedict is an invitation to conscious living. Its wisdom reminds us that God gives every moment, and no activity is so mundane that it cannot reveal divine presence. The sacrament of the present moment applies to work too. This second, this work, these hands performing a task are pregnant with Christ-life waiting to be born in our awareness. I may stand at the sink scouring a pot, impatient because I would prefer to be reading a new book or watching a favorite TV program, when I hear a whisper: "The sacrament of the present moment." I slow down, let go of resentment, continue my work with care and find gratitude beginning to grow as I think of the meal cooked in that pot and of the abundance with which I am blessed. The awareness of God's providence leads me to intercession for the vast numbers of hungry people on this planet and to a question about ways in which I might reach out to the needy in my own community.

In a culture oriented toward leisure, we tend to undervalue work or to value it solely as a means of making money. Feelings of resentment about ordinary, unexciting tasks can increase, especially when such tasks seem to steal time we would rather use for leisure activities. Many people feel trapped by unrewarding responsibilities and by jobs not valued by others. Benedict invites us to consider work done well and with attention a gift of gratitude to God. He tells us to let go of resentment, to see our tasks as opportunities to express thanksgiving and as a means of service to those around us. Manual labor has value, and bringing in the harvest is no less honorable than creating illuminated manuscripts in the scriptoriam or preaching erudite sermons at community worship.

The challenge today is to allow lessons learned in the monastery to condition our attitudes toward tasks that we often have to do under pressure and without bells calling us to worship. A few days ago I set aside a morning to clear out and update a file cabinet that was bulging with old papers. My project began well enough with a desire that I would allow this not very inspiring but necessary work to be my prayer as I carefully sorted correspondence. For a while I was "present," but then the telephone rang and I needed to deal with a problem; and then a colleague came to the door with a question. As I turned back to the files irritation began to grow, and I did the task mechanically. I entertained thoughts of how much easier things would be if I had more support staff. Then I began to sense an inner voice asking, "Where are you?" and I was called back to the present moment. My body was where it had been all along in Black Mountain, North Carolina, but my mind had drifted into a fantasy world where I could escape the ordinary, unexciting, time-consuming tasks that requested my attention.

One of the ways in which I am slowly learning to experience the sacrament of the present moment is to pray the interruptions, which begins with my acknowledging their presence. A fax arrives or a thought arises that I need to do something about. Instead of worrying or trying to solve the problem right away, perhaps all that is required *now* is that I make a note to deal with the task later. I then return to the present task. If the interruption requires immediate attention—a sick child to be picked up from school, an employee needing help with a demanding customer, an elderly neighbor dealing with a power failure—then it is time to move attention to the new task and to be present to its demands. Here too I can consciously let go of what will now remain undone, asking for the grace to be present in the new situation as an agent of God's love.

The second of twelve steps in humility, which Benedict outlines in the Rule, is that we love not our own will nor take pleasure in the satisfaction of our desires; rather we shall imitate by our actions that saying of the Lord: "I have come down from heaven, not to do my own will, but the will of him who sent me" (John 6:38). This self-abnegation applies to work assignments and all other aspects of life together in the monastery. The vow of obedience is designed not to constrict or diminish a monk but to teach him that self-centered preferences are a refusal to embrace the Christian ideal of interdependence. They deny the basic truth that we need each other, a truth proclaimed by Paul to the divided church in Corinth:

> Just as the body is one and has many members, and all the members of the body, though many, are one body, so it is with

Christ.…Indeed, the body does not consist of one member but of many. If the foot would say, "Because I am not a hand, I do not belong to the body," that would not make it any less a part of the body.… Now you are the body of Christ and individually members of it (1 Cor. 12:12, 14-15, 27).

Work as Service

In a healthy body, all limbs and organs function well, serving one another and promoting wholeness. Work teaches the Benedictine monk that God created him for a purpose far greater than personal satisfaction and that what he does blesses others. Many of us have few occasions when we participate in work that enables us to see a product or process from beginning to end, which may encourage our disconnection from a sense of interdependence. We see only our little piece of tedious activity. Disconnection may also mean that we fail to value work, our own or other people's, because we find it distasteful or personally unfulfilling. The recovery of a sense of connection and responsibility is a major priority for those who choose to embody Benedictine spirituality.

I remember being asked to help the monks shell field peas one day at the monastery after they had been gathered from the small fenced garden where little grew. I had other "more important" things to do and sat resentfully on the back step trying to use a precarious gadget one of the monks had invented to speed the process. The field peas flew all over the place, and my fingers hurt. At the end of the morning after several hours of labor, I had a small bowl of peas. Because the monks could have bought a package of them at the store and I could have saved myself the effort, I had to be jolted into an awareness of the importance of this work. Two of the monks especially loved field peas, a food my northern palate did not readily appreciate. These men took great delight in eating what had been grown on the property, and their smiles were my reward. I did the assigned task, not with the best grace, but at least with the knowledge that as an oblate I shared the life of the community and its obligations and so did not exist only for myself. In a culture that repeatedly encourages personal fulfillment and fills bookstore shelves with self-help books to support that quest, we need reminders of our communal responsibility.

Recently a local supplier delivered a new dishwasher to replace the old, dysfunctional one that was in place when I bought my house. It should have been a simple task to disconnect the old machine, and we had agreed on a price for installation. As it turned out, the original dishwasher was a portable model, inexpertly plumbed into a water line that ran down through the floor and protruded so that the machine could not be pulled over it. The dealer struggled for two hours, removing pieces of pipe, dismantling sections of the dishwasher, and warning me that he might be unable to complete the installation if expert plumbing became necessary.

However, the dealer did not give up, though it was now Saturday afternoon and past the time he would usually work. Finally he freed the old machine, but he then needed fresh copper pipe to replace what he had cut away. The man left to buy the supplies and to collect additional tools. Three and a half hours after arriving, he completed the task. At no time did he complain or cease to give full attention to the arduous and complicated task. He never suggested that the additional work was beyond his contract; he gave of his best, knowing that his work affected others.

This man's commitment to exceptional service in an age where all too often the sale of a product represents the end of responsibility touched me deeply. His vision of work closely resembles that of Saint Benedict, since he recognizes that what he does and how he does it touches other lives. I know that he values his Christian faith, because when I first called him to my house several years ago to repair an appliance, he told me he was teaching himself New Testament Greek so he could better understand the scriptures. But he does not need to preach in order to bear witness to the gospel; his attentive way of working testifies to all of his care, his affirmation that they matter, and that service, not acquisitiveness, gives direction to life.

"Idleness is the enemy of the soul," says Saint Benedict, and in her book *Friend of the Soul* Norvene Vest writes of work in our contemporary world by inverting the phrase. Work, she tells us, is a friend that enables us to pay loving attention to our soul life as we grow in God. She deals realistically with boring work, with challenges to faith when asked to engage in unethical practice, with relationships that become strained through oppressive personnel policies. I am especially struck by the phrase *tender competence*, which she uses to express the Benedictine attitude to work that we are called upon to embody:

> Tender competence is a difficult practice, because it challenges the base-line myth of contemporary society that one is either firmly in control or completely helpless. Both control and helplessness are ways of excluding God. If we are fully in charge, there is no place for God's action. If we are completely helpless, we refuse not only God's desire to work in our midst, but also the opportunities before us and our own competence to engage in them. Stewardship places outcomes in God's hands, but takes quite seriously the challenge of tender competence in the meanwhile.[4]

I saw this tender competence in the man who viewed the problem of installing my dishwasher as an opportunity for service. I would like to approach work-related difficulties with the same trust that God will use my faithfulness as the means by which things are changed. In this way work is befriended and becomes prayer, leading us deeper into God's call to serve.

A JOURNAL ENTRY

March 15, 1996

This morning my body hurts, and I am aware of having little time to do all that lies ahead. I hear God asking me to be present and use this high-pressure time as an invitation to grow. Yesterday was long, filled with tension at the office and included a meeting with a committee chairperson who is becoming dysfunctional. At our staff meeting we heard from a critical, dissatisfied church leader who came to challenge some of our practices. Nothing was resolved. I went to a concert last night, which meant I got to bed late, and I was up early to deal with the chimney sweep, the furnace repair man, and a guest needing breakfast. So . . . I look out of the window, and nothing has changed. As I read today's scriptures the image of God as a Rock predominates. I need stability and the grace to be in the present, especially when it is distasteful. I take the words of Psalm 61:2 as my prayer: "Set me upon the rock that is higher than I." May my work be done in God's strength.

GOD OF CREATION, help me participate in your work with tender competence and gratitude that the offering of my hands, heart, and mind may bless others. Amen.

Suggestions for Reflection

1. Scripture passage for *lectio divina*: 2 Thessalonians 3:6-13.

2. Identify a work activity that you find distasteful, and choose a scripture phrase to repeat silently as you engage in the task: "*Maranatha* (Our Lord, come)," "Bless the work of my hands," "Renew a right spirit within me," "Behold it is very good."

3. Recall times when your work has brought you joy and satisfaction. How might you express your gratitude and celebrate work as friend? In what ways might you reach out to someone who lacks the dignity of work?

SIX

REST

❦

After Sext and their meal,
they may rest on their beds in complete silence;
should a brother wish to read privately, let him do so,
but without disturbing the others.[1]

O N A GREY, COLD British morning early in 1982 a small
group of clergy gathered with the Dean of Saint Paul's Cathedral
for a simple service of Holy Communion. I had recently
returned to my native England as a newly ordained priest in
the Anglican Communion, and the Dean had invited me to
celebrate the Eucharist in his home.

The previous months had been filled with feverish activity—preparing for the ordination, receiving friends who crossed
the Atlantic to share the occasion, dealing with media repre-
sentatives who wanted to create headline stories because I was
the first woman from the Church of England to become a priest
in the Episcopal Church, after specifically leaving "home" to
do so. Four TV companies had been present in Newark Cathedral for the ordination, and my British bishop, unable to ordain
me in England, had flown to the United States to preach and
to join in the act of consecration. It had been a breathless time
of excitement, hope, and fulfillment. I had returned to England
for what I thought would be a rest. Instead I had been swamped

by invitations and requests. I had already celebrated one Eucharist at the Deanery for about fifty supporters of the Movement for the Ordination of Women. At the same time, TV and radio stations besieged me with requests for interviews.

As we gathered in the Dean's home, the clergymen offered me affirmation and hope for a more inclusive Church of England (although women were ordained in several branches of the Anglican Communion, the law of church and land denied them hospitality at the altar in the Church of England). Then one of them, rector of a nearby parish, asked if I had some time to spare following the service. Anxious to respond to the needs of others and to further the "cause," I said yes. Later that morning we walked through the London streets and into the crypt of his centuries-old church. We passed through the Court of Arches that had witnessed ecclesiastical trials of past ages and into a small, sparsely furnished worship space. A plain altar, cross, and muted light drew me into a quiet space, and my friend sat down beside me.

Expecting my friend to ask for something I waited, tense, ready to respond. Instead the silence grew, and I began to sense a loving, prayerful presence as this priest wordlessly invited me into a resting place. When I realized that he was not asking me to provide something but to receive a gift, tears began to flow. In this period of intense activity I had forgotten to stop, to wait, and to be open to the renewing power of restful presence, the Sabbath time with which the Creator gifted humankind at the beginning of all things. Now I received again a glimpse of God's gratuitousness and of my need through the sensitive time offering by another human pilgrim.

That incident stands for me as a reminder of how often God has graced me with rest when I have forgotten, after the model of the Creator on the seventh day, to schedule adequate time for ceasing from labor. Sometimes the gift comes to me through sickness that follows exhaustion, a sickness that compels me to rest with aching bones and congested nasal passages and to repent of the self-willed drivenness that denied space for recreation. Sometimes I receive the gift through a sudden cancellation of several appointments that leaves time for play, reflection, and renewal. But above all, these graced moments invite me to take seriously the divine gift of rest and to set a high value on creating time to receive and enjoy it. These Sabbath moments offer me the opportunity to let go of the messages of childhood, which represented the Sabbath as a heavy obligation; a day of demand, denial, and dismal duty. Instead these gratuitous moments remind me that God gives a divine pattern of work and rest for my health and pleasure. I impoverish myself if I fail to receive gratefully the rest that wraps itself around all my doings.

Rest Reflecting Divine Rhythms

Saint Benedict was clear about the need to provide monks with adequate time for rest from the labor of prayer and manual work. During siesta time all were to rest undisturbed, replenishing both body and soul in gentle relaxation. Benedict says that anyone who chooses to read during this time must do so quietly so as not to interrupt others, an insightful glimpse into the ancient practice of reading scripture aloud; no one had yet realized that the eyes alone might peruse the written word! There is something important for us here. I notice that when I read aloud, I slow down; I listen more deeply; I hear nuances that I often miss in the fast visual scanning of a text. When it does not disturb another person, I try to remember to read this way, thus to hear God speak the word more clearly to my heart.

Rhythm is a keynote in the Rule of Saint Benedict. The many details of times for prayer, meals, work, recreation, and community gatherings may sound tedious to us, but they made a great deal of sense for people seeking balance in their lives. Resonance, or balance, characterized life together so that too much work exhausted no one nor did anyone suffer lethargy through inactivity. There was balance too among the needs of body, mind, and spirit. In the daily routine, as well as in the changing seasons and liturgical year, structures provided for the wholeness and well-being of each person. In our fast-paced, often driven lifestyle, we may glean much wisdom from the Benedictine way.

One of the problems for those of us who have absorbed the predominant tenets of Western theological thought is that we have learned to think of God as *actus purus*—pure activity— and to forget the many biblical references to God's resting. As a consequence we think of ourselves as reflecting the divine image through our activity; and if we have also imbibed the Protestant work ethic, there is little awareness of the sacredness of rest. Our culture also colludes with compulsive inclinations by rewarding us for achievement, financial success, upward mobility in career structures, and never being idle. We are encouraged to participate in competitive games or to observe others doing so. Vendors of mind-numbing escapes attempt to alleviate our frenzied activity, but few models for reflective, recreative rest exist. The biblical invitation to enter into the rest promised by God is, in itself, an antidote to driven consumerism and a gift to restore the fullness of the divine image in which God made us.

The author of Hebrews offers many parallels between the need for rest during the pilgrimage of God's ancient people and and that of the Christian community now addressed. The author also gives frequent warnings and promises based on the experience of journey and resting places. Foundational to human wholeness is the model of the Creator who rested on the seventh day from *every* work. The Hebrew Scriptures are filled with references to honoring the Sabbath. However, keeping the Sabbath in itself does not cause the Hebrews to enter God's rest any more than my punctilious "no sewing on Sunday" and other taboos in my youth enabled me to experience the gift of rest. Why? Because faith is lacking; stopping becomes a duty severed from relationship with God. So the author of Hebrews calls Christians to remember that rest still remains for God's people. Sometimes, however, we have to work hard in order to enter it! "Let us therefore make every effort to enter that rest, so that no one may fall through such disobedience as theirs" (Heb. 4:11).

Scheduling Rest

For me the "hard work" of entering into rest begins with taking my calendar seriously. I am always tempted to think I can squeeze in one more appointment, schedule another meeting, or go to more events. The one thing I forget to schedule, or to keep absolutely sacred when I do write it in, is rest. In fact I derive a certain sense of satisfaction from being overbusy, so much in demand, so involved in ministry. There is a subtle arrogance in the failure to claim rest—I am so important I have no time for rest—and a collusion with the contemporary world that rewards busy-ness but neglects rest time for and with the Creator. Recently I realized that I had not taken a time of retreat in a long time. I rearranged my calendar and went for thirty-six hours to a monastic house, where the rhythm of prayer and no responsibility for answering the telephone provided me with a space in which to rest. I walked, prayed, read, slept, and spent several hours planning my calendar for the next eight months. I scheduled one day off each week, as well as a five-day retreat. I also set aside one day a month for retreat when I would get away from routine in order to listen and rest with God. As pressures build I may find it difficult to honor this commitment, but planning rest in my schedule is a beginning.

Companions on the Way

God not only offers us the gift of rest but calls us into community. The Israelites journeyed together, sharing the stops and starts, sometimes grumbling, sometimes forgetting the reason for their travels and the need to rest. At various times God raised up individuals to offer encouragement, challenge, and a retelling of history so that the people might remember their call. At its best the Christian community supports our individual faith journeys and, even at its worst, reminds us that we are among other vulnerable, fallible believers trying to grow more Christlike in our discipleship.

Our weekly gathering for worship recalls the need for rest, reminds us that God asks for a central place in our lives, and offers forgiveness for our failures, encouragement on the way, and grace to keep us from giving up. We need one another and the accountability that membership in the church, the body of Christ, implies. Some of us make that accountability more intentional through relationship with a spiritual director who helps us stay honest, prods, encourages, and enables us to prioritize the need for rest. I know that I will need this support if I am to keep my plans for rest.

Our lives get lopsided when we stuff them with too much activity, so packed down with things to do that we have no time to be. My five years as a Benedictine oblate taught me the value of monastic rhythms, and since leaving that community I have struggled to embody the main tenets of the Rule as I juggle the demands of ministry in the world. I am beginning to understand why today so many people outside the cloister are finding that Benedict speaks to their needs and offers principles that enable more wholistic living in the world. From time to time Stillpoint hosts "Benedictine Days" in which people gather for twelve hours and live an adapted form of the Rule together. We observe the Daily Offices, celebrate Eucharist, take time out for study of scripture and personal prayer, work in the yard, and rest.

For most of us just taking a day out in this way is a rest from our usual patterns of life, but it is important that the day also contain time for rest, for "doing nothing." At the end, after a sung Vespers in which we often attempt some simple plainsong chant, we reflect on the experience. One participant said that the main lesson of the day had been to realize how unbalanced her daily routine usually was. She recognized a need to do more than take off one day a week; she needed to receive God's gift of rest at some point each day and to respond gratefully to it.

In her book *Seeking God: The Way of Saint Benedict*, Esther de Waal reminds us that while good order and stability of the community are the *means*, the *end* is to offer each individual space and time to enter into personal dialogue with God. I experienced this aspect of Christian community with the Anglican rector who shared some "spare" time with me. My newfound friend, who gifted me with time to be when I had forgotten my need for silence, enabled me to become still enough to listen to God once again. The dialogue was able to continue, a dialogue that allowed for *hearing* what Creator-God wanted to say and for stopping some of my babbling. The gift of rest, received from another struggling human who all too often found himself trying to balance the heavy demands of a large-city parish and the need for personal time to pray, transformed the remainder of my time in England. I even heard myself say no once in a while.

One of the suggested scripture readings contained in the beautiful late-night service of Compline is the invitation of Jesus: "Come to me, all you that are weary and are carrying heavy burdens, and I will give you rest. Take my yoke upon you, and learn from me; for I am gentle and humble in heart, and you will find rest for your souls. For my yoke is easy, and my burden is light" (Matt. 11:28-30). This invitation seems an entirely appropriate way to end the day. As we let go of the busy-ness, the fragmentedness, the weariness, we pause to ask ourselves how far we have lived out of that gentle humility that Christ displayed and that we too will know as we are "yoked" to him.

Echoing the words of Jesus, Benedict said that he wanted to offer "nothing harsh, nothing burdensome" to his monks. Jesus struggled to take time out from his ministry to replenish his tired spirit, to continue the dialogue with his Father. Our choosing to follow Jesus means we accept the discipline of doing the same. This discipline feels like a burden that requires some effort, but it also enables us to receive the gift and so becomes lighter as we shoulder it. God graces us with rest; and, as we respond with our gratitude and receive the gift, we begin to enter that balanced life that is our destiny as the people of a loving Creator.

A Journal Entry

May 29, 1996

"The world is charged with the grandeur of God"
(Gerard Manley Hopkins)..."There is a dawn in me"
(Henry David Thoreau)...sun gentles my face...water
trickles...birds are abundant and speak abundantly...the
Creator sets before me a day full of mystery, full of treasure to be mined from every moment and encounter. I
desire mindfulness, the awakened state that rouses me
from half-living and allows me to be deeply aware of the
dynamic potential and gift of today.

"Listen to the stones of the wall" (Thomas
Merton)...the wood thrush...your life...listen with the
ear of your heart to the rhythms of grace, returning,
renewing, restoring. Wait for the whisper that weaves
calm among the clamorous lust to fix, avoid, overcome,
succeed. Today the Gospel reading is Luke 14:25-33, the
parable about a king going out to battle but first estimat-
ing the cost before deciding to wage war. If he is not
strong enough, he will seek terms of peace instead of
fighting. Which of your enemies are too big for you to
fight? What terms of peace may sustain you in hope?
Hope is the Creator's gift; play comes to invite a child's
joy, a mystic imagination that longs to dance with you
through the day. Come. It is time to begin, and the world
is your playground.

Loving God, you spoke to your ancient people saying, "In
returning and rest you will be saved; in quietness and trust shall
be your strength." Grant that we too may find grace to cease
from busy-ness and be still in your presence. Let our restless

hearts find their true rest in you and restore our tired minds. Enable us, by your Holy Spirit, to defeat the enemies of fear, envy, anxiety, and impatience that drive us to exhaustion, and give to us that peace which the world can never give. We pray in the name of Jesus, Prince of Peace. Amen.

SUGGESTIONS FOR REFLECTION

1. Scripture passage for *lectio divina*: Mark 6:30-32.

2. Look at your calendar for the next few days and intentionally schedule a time for rest; do not be discouraged if you find that a day or several hours are not available. Start small, but be faithful to the time you have. What would be most restful for you? Walking in the woods? Taking a long bubble bath? Lying in a hammock? Playing with the dog? Finding a quiet spot for "doing nothing"? Celebrate the gift of rest, offering this recreative time to the Creator, who knew when to stop!

3. Consider whether you might be able to offer the gift of rest to another. Perhaps you could provide childcare so that a busy mother might have some time off or give respite to a caregiver who constantly tends a sick spouse. Do you know an overbusy executive for whom you could model the importance of time out? Might you introduce family rest time at home, an evening when you "do nothing" together? Incorporate the need for rest into prayer so that you are alert to ways in which you can claim rest time and encourage others to do the same.

SEVEN

STABILITY

*Do not grant newcomers to the monastic life
an easy entry, but, as the Apostle says,* Test the spirits
to see if they are from God *(1 John 4:1)....
If he promises perseverance in his stability, then after two
months have elapsed let this rule be read straight through
to him, and let him be told: "This is the law under
which you are choosing to serve. If you can keep it,
come in. If not, feel free to leave."* [1]

THE THREEFOLD VOW that Benedictine monastics take differs somewhat from the more common monastic vows of poverty, chastity, and obedience, although it embodies the same intent. Stability, conversion of life, and obedience are the promises that Saint Benedict asks of those who would join the community, promises that readily translate into life outside the cloister. As Christians who live in a global village where mobility is the norm, where people frequently are uprooted geographically, and where faithfulness in relationships is threatened constantly, a life of inner stability becomes a priority. Called to live like the displaced Christ whom we follow, we find our choices cause us to be countercultural and always vigilant lest we fall prey to acquisitiveness and self-interest. Conversion is a daily necessity as we deal with desires, deceptions, and the ever present inclination to compromise our discipleship. And in a time when rights and license to live without regard for the common good predominate, obedience asks us to act as God expects whether we like it or not. "No one tells me what to do" is the cry of many today. "Listen with the ear of your heart," says Saint Benedict, "for the Lord waits for us daily to translate into action, as we should, his holy teachings."[2] The obedience that follows listening provides the foundation for Christian disciples.

The stability that Benedict calls for asks us to live in the "now"—to be present to this moment whether pleasurable or painful. We are part of a culture where escape from every kind of discomfort is to be found through access to a pill, a therapy, or some mindless entertainment. So we are encouraged never to stay with the uncomfortable experience long enough to ask what it means and where we might find God in it.

My first reaction to a headache is to swallow my favorite pain medication so the pain will go away. But wait a minute— before I self-medicate, maybe I need to ask what caused my disease; maybe there is some lesson here, some word from God. Have I been frenetically pushing the limits, rushing from one place to another, taking on too many responsibilities because I favor rewards for my busy-ness?

When I choose to stop and reflect, I may hear a gracious word from God that asks me to look at this behavior in light of the need for balance and care for myself. If I pause long enough to recognize destructive, obsessive patterns, I may well be led from that stable moment to conversion as I repent of the arrogant choices that support my self-image of indispensability.

Stability lies in slowing down, being willing to wait, going on with the sameness that is an inevitable part of being human and refusing the quick-fix alternative. One of the desert fathers, asked by a young monk for a word to help him on the spiritual path, replied, "Go to your cell and your cell will teach you everything." Be where you are. Refuse the fantasy world of "if only." Remember that discipleship is about faithful living, not visible success. Be prepared to wait, sometimes a long time, to hear the word of God that tells you it is time to move on.

Stability as Waiting

Waiting is one of the most difficult and most divine aspects of our experience. We find waiting difficult because it reminds us that we have not arrived, that we are unfinished, and that the present moment is one in which to live the "not yet" of faith. And waiting frequently becomes more difficult when compounded by our fear of what may be or by our doubt that waiting will result in joy. But waiting is also God-like. Scripture bears witness to the God who waits again and again for the right moment to act in the life of a community or an individual. That waiting is especially poignant as God takes flesh in the body of a young woman and becomes subject to the nine months of pregnancy. God's waiting affects us, and often we interpret it as inaction on the part of the Creator to whom we cry out. As we deal with the feelings generated by the sense that nothing is happening, our prayer and faith grow and we test our stability.

The psalms the Benedictine monastics recite daily often allude to waiting, offering us a way to pray the distress ("waiting for") as well as the trust ("waiting on") that comes as we live in the between times of unfulfilled hope. When life's problems consume us or pain racks our bodies, we may want to pray the words of Psalm 77:9—"Has God forgotten to be gracious? Has he in anger shut up his compassion?"—for we really do entertain thoughts of abandonment. Psalm 22:1-2 expresses even more acutely that sense of being forgotten:

> My God, my God, why have you forsaken me?
>   Why are you so far from helping me,
>   from the words of my groaning?
> O my God, I cry by day, but you do not answer;
>   and by night, but find no rest.

These real prayers, uttered by persons overwhelmed by the badness of life and the nonanswers of a silent God, eloquently express their feelings.

Alongside these expressions of despair we find prayers of hope and thanksgiving as the psalmists learn to wait patiently, trusting that God still cares.

> For God alone my soul waits in silence;
>   from him comes my salvation.
>   —Psalm 62:1

This verse expresses the confidence of one who, while aware of oppressive enemies all around, has learned to wait quietly in the presence of the Creator who alone can save. The writer of Psalm 130, after crying to God from the depths, says,

> I wait for the Lord, my soul waits,
>   and in his word I hope;
> my soul waits for the Lord
>   more than those who watch for the morning" (vv. 5-6).

This prayer reflects an alert anticipation, a waiting on God in hopeful trust by one who has consented to be present in the waiting instead of consumed by the tentative quality of life.

I find myself praying in both of these forms, sometimes asking God why there seems to be no end to the waiting, no answer

to my questions, no relief from my fears. But I also pray as one
who has experienced the compassion of God in the past and
who finds in those earlier times of renewal a reason for trusting the future. Often the prayer of confidence and trust follows
the cry of anguish, for in the expression of pain I consent to be
honest with God, confessing the limitations of my faith and
finding, like Thomas, that the One I thought was gone now
stands before me. When I willingly live the now of distress,
grace reaches out to me and bathes my distress in the light of
God's compassion.

The motivation for joining a monastery lies largely in the
desire to belong, to live with like-minded persons for whom
prayer is central. We all yearn for a sense of community; we
want to be at home, yet, paradoxically, the commitment to follow Jesus Christ causes us to feel displaced. We become, as the
author of Hebrews tells us, "strangers and foreigners on the
earth" (Heb. 11:13) like our many forebears in the faith, who
sought a homeland but knew that it lay in a better country, a
heavenly one. Whether inside the monastic enclosure or "in
the world," God's people are always on pilgrimage, which often
means dealing with loss of the comfortable and familiar. Unless
we develop an inner stability that keeps us centered on the
unchanging love of God, we will find ourselves out of kilter,
stumbling along and tempted to reach for the first painkiller
that helps us to forget.

A monk, sent by the abbot to a new location just when he
has begun to feel comfortable in his current setting, feels
uprooted, resentful, angry. He may choose the pill of self-pity,
refusing to see opportunity for growth in the new place. A
woman finds the courage to leave an abusive marriage, and,
because the aloneness is so new and painful, she may fall too
quickly into another unhealthy relationship to fill the void. A

young undergraduate begins studies, enjoying the first months away from home and determined to bear witness to faith in Jesus Christ among her peers. She chooses a hard road, trying to resist pressure to join others at all night parties that take away sleep and study time, to use the "soft" drugs that make her feel good for a short time; but she finally may succumb out of a desire for acceptance and belonging. Each of these persons may become engaged in the fruitless attempt to avoid a sense of exile, because dealing with the present moment out of a place of inner stability is such hard work.

Living with Loss

When I left England in 1981 I began a journey of self-imposed exile with much sadness at the loss of home but also filled with hopeful anticipation as the fulfillment of my call drew near. In the first months I stayed busy planning the ordination, adjusting to full-time parish ministry, meeting new friends, and enjoying the novelty of living in a new country. When my first temporary appointment came to an end, I moved to New York City to complete further graduate studies and to look for a new position. Only then, more than a year after I had left England, did I begin to experience a genuinely painful sense of loss and to feel that I did not really belong in that teeming, vibrant, exciting, and tough city. With meager financial resources, no permanent parish appointment, and now distant from the new friends I had made in New Jersey, I felt lonely and dislocated. Who was I? Had the move to the U.S. been a mistake? Would I ever be able to integrate with this culture? Would people want what I had to offer, or would I join the ranks of unemployed clergy? Where was God?

I began to record my fear and disappointment, not in the

form of a psalm, but in daily journal entries in which I now see overwhelming fear and bits of paranoia. I remembered the clarity with which I had chosen to move to the United States, and occasionally I remembered God's grace in past times of loss. God gifted me at this time with a series of vivid dreams that I recorded and in which I found much wisdom as I reflected on their meaning. I probably would not have been receptive to the message, "Wait patiently for God," but I could begin to see more clearly that the feeling of oppression and abandonment might not last forever. Some of my fear stemmed from reality; and I understood the present situation as one to be lived through, not avoided with some unconscious escape or denied through pious platitudes. As I cried out, "How long, O God?" somehow the waiting for answers became more tolerable, and I learned to make little commitments of trust that took far more effort than the big decision to cross the Atlantic.

One of the dreams helped with the "Who am I?" question. I dreamed that I was producing a play, but the actors had not learned their lines. I would gather one group and find that they had left their scripts behind, and those who wanted to begin had parts that came much later in the play. Then a small goat walked onstage. Someone pointed to it and said, "You know, you should give her a much bigger part; she's very talented." I realized a child was inside the goatskin, but I dismissed the remark because of my preoccupation with getting the play started. The chaos continued; I again was told to pay attention to the "goat," and then I woke. Little wonder that John A. Sanford has described dreams as "God's forgotten language."[3] With clarity and playfulness God "spoke" to me, for the dream accurately reflected my chaotic feelings of disorder and the sense that I "could not get my act together." Remembering that we participate in as well as observe our dreams, I thought about the various characters. I certainly shared a kinship with those who had not yet learned the lines; I had not really adjusted to life in New York City and felt unsure about how to speak my part. At the same time I resembled those anxious to get the play started; my impatience because nothing seemed to be happening made the feelings of exile more acute. But the dream told me it was not yet time for the big scene. Instead, I had to wait out the muddle. And that waiting meant that the whole situation was "getting my goat!"

But perhaps the most important issue came in the invitation to notice the little "kid," the child within who, though talented, now doubted her ability to be of use. I had to hear that message twice before I took it in. Through that dream I started learning to be in exile. Over the next few months I learned to connect with the stories of other exiles, God's people in Babylon hanging their harps upon the willows by the water, learning to sing the Lord's song on alien soil (Ps. 137); Jacob, fleeing from home and family, finding God through the dream given him as he journeyed that prepared him for the return many years later; Esther, a Hebrew woman exiled in the harem of the Persian king, confronting her fear, stepping outside cultural gender expectations, and saving her people from extinction. The experience of exile, though painful, became the crucible in which faith was refined in them, and the faithfulness of God was made known to future generations.

Finding God in Chaos

During that first year in New York City, I learned that stability meant staying faithful to my regular rhythm of prayer, allowing the disorientation simply to be, and resisting the resentment. I also learned that the experience of chaos does not necessarily come about because we have caused it. Certainly my choices had placed me in New York City, but the consequences of those choices might have been very different, so I need not have engaged in self-blame. It also dawned on me that chaos and darkness are places where God chooses to be present. In the first creation story (Genesis 1), God's spirit moves over the dark, chaotic void; then God speaks to bring order and life. At the beginning of Saint John's Gospel, Jesus the Word enters darkness to give life, empowering those who receive him to become children of God. And into my chaos Christ walked through a dream and gave me the grace to be where I was.

Some of the old gospel hymns contain great wisdom. "Count your blessings, name them one by one," advises one song, going on to say that what the Lord has done will surprise us. How true that is. One of the most positive ways to end the day—even the worst of days—is to pause and consider where thanksgiving is appropriate in our lives. We may begin by being grateful for such basic things as breath, adequate food, shelter, the capacity for thought, gradually becoming aware of little, unnoticed events that brought joy during a day that may have seemed routine. The smile of the woman at the check-out counter; the first crocus in bud, evidence of approaching spring; the scripture verse that came to mind; the memory of some act of kindness on the part of a neighbor—all these, as they are recalled, begin to change our perspective on life and on God. Remembering makes the waiting time more bearable, for it fills the present emptiness with hope and allows God to be bigger than the present moment might suggest.

One old gospel song says, "I love to tell the story of unseen things above," and suggests the importance of the role of the community in keeping alive an awareness of God's action in human history. The psalms, whether written by an individual dealing with some intensely personal experience or for corporate liturgical use, represent a vibrant and compelling call to remember and to celebrate the involvement of God in sacred history by telling the stories over and over again. As we hear the stories, we find our own experience writ large, which encourages us to go on in trust and hope. Often God gives us others to share our story, the community functioning fully as we not only celebrate moments of grace but learn to share one another's burdens and so fulfill the law of Christ. And always journaling the journey keeps us in touch with hope.

Waiting patiently on God becomes possible as we tune in to the word of God that addresses us in our need. Recently I pondered a verse from Psalm 46: "The Lord of hosts is with us; the God of Jacob is our refuge" (v. 7). I needed to enter into a place of confidence and to receive strength for the day in which I anticipated some difficult decisions and meetings. I experienced this verse as a gift from God, repeated it thankfully, and allowed it to become part of my prayer.

Then, as I sat in silence, I became aware of another persistent voice repeating old, discouraging messages in the background. It was a familiar sound that told me life is fragile, the present moment insecure, and the future unpredictable. As the voice spoke, my anxiety grew; fear began to replace confidence in God my Refuge. Then God showed me that I could choose between the two voices; I didn't have to pay attention to the discordant sounds invoking fear. I could remove them from the realm of the unconscious and expose their shrill emptiness for what it truly was. I returned to the awareness of God's loving omnipotence and embraced the call to love and serve the divine purpose.

Daring to journey within and to discover the word of God engraved deeply in our hearts means life. Another voice may try persistently to tell us that God's will means loss, a denial of our greatest longings, and an existence of stoic endurance. These lies keep us from fullness of life and the joy of discovering that in the deepest part of ourselves we are at one with the Creator in what we truly desire. To wait with and on such a God places one in harmony with the cosmos, which is ever waiting, ever coming to fullness. By consenting to wait, we refuse the myth that we are diminished by inactivity, and we announce to the world that God who waits is Creator of all times and seasons. In such waiting we embrace stability, knowing our souls are anchored to Christ the Rock; and we are "grounded firm and deep in the Savior's love."

A JOURNAL ENTRY

1991

"I haven't got time for the pain," they say,
a caplet or shrink
will settle everything—
insomnia, neurosis, constipation—
cherry flavored
oblivion
and a blast of T.V.
first-aiding the forgetting.

Cats know better.
Attentive to the pain
they wait wide-eyed
and watch,
curled and still
they let the hurting be
and, wiser than humans,
yield themselves to now.

Pain asks for time,
requests our presence
and teaches us the measure of our joy.
We drink the bitter cup
and angels bear us
through the dark night of our unknowing
into the Easter moment.

GOD OF LIFE, you always meet us in the present moment but sometimes we pass you by in our effort to get somewhere else. Heal our unfaithfulness and open our eyes to see and our hands to receive the grace you wait to give. Strengthen us to walk with you until we know you revealed in scripture and the breaking of bread. Amen.

SUGGESTIONS FOR REFLECTION

1. Scripture passage for *lectio divina*: Matthew 7:24-27.

2. Sit down with your journal and ask God's Spirit to help you remember those times when you have experienced being grounded in God. Begin to write briefly of those occasions, naming the blessings that came as you trusted that you were not alone, particularly in a time of turbulence. Ask yourself where God invites you to live stability in the present. One helpful way to do this is to look for the inclination to escape or ignore an uncomfortable situation.

3. Pick up your favorite hymnal and find hymns that sustain and help you stay faithful in your Christian discipleship. You might sing some of them, at home or walking in the country, not worrying about the quality of voice or tone but making a "joyful noise to the Lord." Whom might you encourage through a word, poem, psalm, hymn in dealing with a situation of instability?

EIGHT

CONVERSION OF LIFE

*The Lord waits for us daily to translate
into action, as we should, his holy teachings.
Therefore our life span has been lengthened by way
of a truce, that we may amend our misdeeds.
As the Apostle says: Do you not know that the patience
of God is leading you to repent? (Rom. 2:4)*[1]

CONVERSION STANDS IN COUNTERPOISE to the vow of stability; Benedict knows that as we grow in the life of faith, grounded in Christ, we become increasingly aware of areas of life we need to change. The monastery is not a place where those who are already perfect live in perpetual harmony but an organic community subject to the struggles that beset every person. Often as people of varying dispositions and diverse personal histories try to live together in the fishbowl intimacy of religious community, these struggles intensify. For this reason the Rule makes provision for dealing with faults that hurt others and calls for frequent personal self-examination that allows the individual monk constantly to return to God for healing and forgiveness.

Saint Benedict is not afraid to talk about sin and to name human failings. In a day when we tend to explain and excuse, his plain talk permeated by scripture references is refreshing. We are not asked to wallow in guilt or engage in belittling who we are but truly to know ourselves always in the presence of an all-seeing, all-loving God who calls us to repentance. Our self-will frequently leads us into ways that distance us from our Creator, but the return home is always a celebration of grace and a feast of delight. Creating rituals to welcome home the prodigal is important. The community ceremonially welcomes the penitent monk back into full participation. The early Christians saw Lent as a time "when those who, because of notorious sins, had been separated from the body of the faithful, were reconciled by penitence and forgiveness, and restored to the fellowship of the Church."[2]

Rituals of Returning

Some years ago I participated in an Ash Wednesday ritual created by an ecumenical group of laypersons and clergy. We met in a large sitting room at a convent in New York City. Chairs were arranged in a circle, and people quietly entered the space. On a coffee table in the center a candle burned. Beside it was a large copper container filled with dried palm leaves and a smaller bowl for incense. No words were spoken, but gentle flute music invited us into reflective waiting. When all had entered the circle, we listened to scripture read by different voices, with enough pauses to allow us to ponder the meaning:

> Yet even now, says the Lord,
>   return to me with all your heart,
> with fasting, with weeping, and with mourning;

rend your hearts and not your clothing.
Return to the Lord, your God,
    for he is gracious and merciful (Joel 2:12-13).

Bless the Lord, O my soul,
    and all that is within me,
    bless his holy name....who forgives all your iniquity,
    who heals all your diseases (Ps. 103:1, 3).

We are ambassadors for Christ, since God is making his appeal through us; we entreat you on behalf of Christ, be reconciled to God (2 Cor. 5:20).

I will get up and go to my father, and I will say to him, "Father, I have sinned against heaven and before you" (Luke 15:18).

As the readings ended, someone reminded us of the joyful processions of the last Palm Sunday when we had walked, like those in the Gospel, waving branches to welcome Christ, the long-awaited Savior. Then we had watched as the dried palms burned to ashes, a powerful reminder of how quickly our fresh songs of praise dry on our lips as we tend to the daily cares and preoccupations of our lives. The pungent reminder of our forgetfulness, unfaithfulness, and lack of trust lingered in the air as we now turned our chairs outward so that we no longer faced one another. The overhead light was extinguished, and the flickering candle threw our shadows onto the walls, reminding us of those hidden deviations and deceptions we needed to acknowledge and confess. The act of turning our backs to one another served as an uncomfortable reminder of the many times when self-interest had triumphed over compassionate caring for our neighbors. We took time to sit with our shame and to confess silently each remembered betrayal of Christ in our failure to respond lovingly to God, others, and ourselves.

We were familiar with receiving ashes on our foreheads as a symbol of repentance and recognition of mortality, but now we were invited to take responsibility by placing the ashes on ourselves. The bowl passed around the circle, and the grey palm dust marked our owning of sin. We prayed for forgiveness. When all had received the ashes, we again turned our chairs inward. We heard the words of absolution pronounced, and the room once more flooded with light. During the singing that followed, those who wished to do so placed grains of incense on burning coals to symbolize prayers of thanksgiving rising to celebrate God's forgiving grace.

Ritual plays a central role in human experience. From the small daily patterns we create for ourselves (and repeat again and again) to the major political, cultural, and religious ceremonies that mark seasons of our lives, we often ritualize what we choose to remember. Sometimes, however, the ritual ceases to impact us because we have forgotten its meaning, and it becomes little more than a tired pageant. We need vision and vigilance to preserve not only those outer expressions of who we are but their inner transformative energy. The Ash Wednesday service in which I participated came about because a group of believers, mostly laypersons, spent time asking how best to express our tradition of observing the beginning of Lent through meaningful action. We expressed our acute awareness of our need for reconciliation and our willingness to change by creating outward symbols of the "right spirit," which we asked God to implant within us as we retraced our journey home.

God Calls Us Home

Saint Benedict clearly understands that following the way of Christ is a challenge that often we fail to meet, wandering aimlessly along byways of self-deception. The Greek term *metanoia* (originally used in military contexts when a battalion was called to right-about-turn) aptly summarizes our call to conversion. We become aware of some place where change is necessary; we stop, and we reverse our direction. God is always calling us home, and Benedict tells us,

> The labor of obedience will bring you back to him from whom you had drifted through the sloth of disobedience. This message of mine is for you, then, if you are ready to give up your own will, once and for all, and armed with the strong and noble weapons of obedience to do battle for the true King, Christ the Lord.[3]

The Hebrew word *teshuvah*, "returning," summarizes the way to God that includes restoration of a damaged or broken relationship. References to God's invitation to return fill the scriptures, as well as many examples of the ritual events that marked Israel's acknowledgment of the central importance of repentance. That acknowledgment finds its fullest expression in the solemn ceremonial of the Day of Atonement, or Yom Kippur, during which participants "remake" themselves by repentance. Vivian George Simmons, a former minister of the West London Synagogue, expresses the inner meaning of Yom Kippur:

> On the Day of Atonement, our arrogance, our self-will, our sense of independence, our worldliness drop from us "like a garment." In the solemn thought of the great poet Gabirol, each Israelite is pictured standing before God on this day: "I am bare and destitute of good works and Thy righteousness alone is my covering." Thus does the Jew face himself and his God on Yom Kippur with humility, yet with confidence and hope.[4]

The journey away from God begins when persons make their achievements the measuring rod by which they judge all else.

The call to return shifts attention to God and demands effort so that we engage imagination, humility, and will. The Hebrew Scriptures illuminate universal human experience when they speak of the constant need for repentance and return in light of our inclination to choose our own "stiff-necked" way. Those of us in the Christian tradition also need ways to express repentance as we find ourselves resisting the kind of discipleship demanded by our baptism into Christ. Central to our faith is the reconciliation initiated by God, who recreates us:

> If anyone is in Christ, there is a new creation: everything old has passed away; see, everything has become new! All this is from God, who reconciled us to himself through Christ, and has given us the ministry of reconciliation (2 Cor. 5:17-18).

This is good news! It brings hope and gives focus to grace. But we do not always live a reconciled life. We too fall back into arrogant self-righteousness; we forget to pray, to love, and to embrace those who are different; we make ourselves once again the center of the universe and cease to live gratefully in God's hospitable world. And oftentimes our Ash Wednesdays, our weekly general confessions in church, and even our personal recitation of sins become more a form than an expression of deep humility and neediness. We cling to the structures but lose the substance.

The Sacrament of Reconciliation

One of the gifts the church extends to us is the opportunity to participate in the sacrament of reconciliation as a way of marking our moments of returning to God. Sometimes called confession, or in earlier times penance, Christians who previously considered this means of grace an inappropriate intrusion into their personal relationship with God now embrace it. I grew up in a denominational context that condemned auricular confession as an empty ritual and an affront to the conviction that we have "one mediator between God and humankind, Christ Jesus, himself human, who gave himself a ransom for all" (1 Tim. 2:5). Those who went to confession were caricatured as people who had not really grasped the gospel and so depended on a priest in a dark box to dispense forgiveness. They spoke their list of sins, received some perfunctory penance such as saying the rosary—we did not really know what that meant but knew it had to do with Mary, who was also suspect—and then left to go on with life as before.

Undoubtedly for some the rite had become a form devoid of the desire for inner transformation, the priest a substitute for the personal struggle to know and grow in Christ. Reconciliation, like any other ritual, can lose its power to renew if we neglect the hard work of coming to know ourselves through daily, prayerful reflection on our response to a loving God who constantly calls us to truth. But I have learned that I based my misunderstanding of the sacrament of reconciliation on unexamined prejudice. This sacrament can be for us a wonderful means of grace that bring healing, encouragement, and strength as well as help us be honest with ourselves and God.

In the early to mid-sixties the Second Vatican Council blew through the Roman Catholic Church, bringing new life to many traditional forms of worship. The changes included greater emphasis on reconciliation as a rite, in which priest and penitent met face to face so as to exchange open conversation and counsel. In many ways this ritual demanded more of both, involving trust and vulnerability and releasing them from anonymity. Absolution included the laying on of hands, symbolizing God's spirit of healing, an action previously impossible when a small grilled window separated the two. The new rite encouraged a greater sense of shared humanity and of the church's role in making us all one in Christ. The Episcopal Church in the United States, which has always offered the sacrament of reconciliation to those who desire it, included two liturgical forms of the rite for the first time in the new *Book of Common Prayer*, 1979. The Lutheran Church makes sacramental reconciliation available to its members, and in various forms members of the so-called "nonliturgical" churches seek ways to celebrate God's forgiveness as two Christians meet together in a confessional context. I write out of this context with appreciation for those graced moments when I have either heard another speak the words of absolution that restore me to intimacy with God or have spoken them to one welcomed home by a loving Creator.

Reflection, self-examination, honesty, and trust are necessary in order to open our hearts to God, who waits to put a right spirit within us. Making confession of who we are begins with reflective silence, a time of attentive listening that helps us understand where we have fallen short of our call to live the Christ-life. Recognizing attitudes and actions we need to own in our confession becomes less difficult if our daily routine includes some form of reflection. A simple form of the Ignatian "Examen" helps me think through my responses to grace each day as I offer them up in my nightly prayer.[5] Self-examination takes place in the "Examen" but also at other times set aside for that purpose. In the past, catalogues of sins to check before going to confession were sometimes offered. But such lists can shortcut our responsibility to wait upon God with the prayer:

Search me, O God, and know my heart;
    try me and know my restless thoughts.

Look well whether there be any wickedness in me
and lead me in the way that is everlasting.
—Psalm 139:22-23, BCP

Listening to God's word through scripture and asking for insight
to know how we have measured up to the invitation to grow
in relationship with God, others, and ourselves becomes more
challenging and real. God, always eager to forgive, always ready
to empower us to live and to change, calls us to conversion.

Being honest with ourselves is not always easy because we
unconsciously filter experience and misread our inclinations.
At this point the compassionate presence of another Christian
can be of utmost value, especially as that person listens us into
our own truth. For many people psychotherapy offers an important means of self-knowledge and growth and perhaps the only
relationship in which they really feel "heard." The therapeutic
process helps uncover hidden motivation, throws light on the
present through exploration of the past, and often explains why
we are the way we are. Frequently we can incorporate the
insights gained through therapy into prayer, especially when
we recognize areas in which we want to change. But there comes
a time when understanding and explaining ourselves are not
enough. We need to take responsibility for who we are and ask
for forgiveness, not explanation. Sacramental confession provides a place for the healing and restoration we desire as we
return to the God who loves us into truth.

The wisdom of a good confessor is of utmost value as we
try to be honest with ourselves and God. Guilt, a very tricky
customer, may be entirely appropriate, but often it attaches
itself to us in situations for which we bear no responsibility
and drags us down by its insidious presence. The conversation
that takes place following confession can help differentiate

between true and false guilt and may remove the burden of unexplored shameful feelings. The trust we place in the one hearing our confession, and the knowledge that anything spoken is inviolate, frees us from the secrets that often make us sick. It calls us into the liberty of being God's children in a world of grace.

The Ash Wednesday shadow on the wall, cast by my own solidity blocking light, generates deep penitence and at the same time a yearning for the "new and right spirit" that God gives. We do not search out our sinfulness in order to indulge in feeling bad but to set ourselves on the path of return. Like the lovable character in the movie *E.T.*, who pointed a glowing finger toward his planet as he uttered his plaintive cry, "Home," we were created with a deep sense of where we belong. Often alienated, sometimes far away, we find the warmth of the God in whose image we have been made touches us; and our hearts respond with desire for homecoming. Always we find a place set for us at the welcoming banquet table.

The Whale Is No Escape!

Conversion is a way of life in the Rule of Saint Benedict because our predisposition to resist God's will means we must change again and again. We yearn for intimacy with God and seek to be God's people in the world but then find ourselves pulled in a different direction by our own desires. Now we want to put distance between ourselves and God, a big distance! I find myself drawn to the story of Jonah because I too want to run away sometimes, and even after numerous acts of repentance I end up pouting sullenly like a thwarted three-year-old! Sometimes I get a glimpse of myself as God sees me and find the grace to smile at my futile attempts to escape grace. Reflection on the Jonah allegory helps me know where I am today on my own journey and to name the fear, prejudice, and faithlessness that drive me.

The story opens with God's word to the prophet: "Go at once to Nineveh, that great city, and cry out against it; for their wickedness has come up before me" (Jonah 1:2). Jonah immediately responds. He sets out to flee to Tarshish from the Lord's presence! Jonah has every reason to resist proclaiming God's word in Nineveh, capital of the Assyrian nation at whose hands the people of Israel have suffered greatly. He embraces the view that any nation other than Israel falls under God's judgment. The author of the Book of Jonah held the contrary conviction, articulated so cogently in Isaiah 40–66, that God's people had a missionary mandate to be "a light to the nations." The story of Jonah thus becomes a kind of tract for the times, challenging exclusive nationalism. Jonah's resistance to the divine call and his attempt to run away confront his contemporaries with their own unwillingness to forgive the past and extend hospitality to those outside the covenant community.

Thomas Merton's journal, written over a five-year period at the Trappist monastery of the Abbey of Gethsemani in Kentucky, was published under the title *The Sign of Jonas.* The prologue "Journey to Nineveh" describes some of his struggles with the vow of stability, which often meant accepting a place and lifestyle that conflicted with his own desire. He writes,

> Like the prophet Jonas, whom God ordered to go to Nineveh, I found myself with an almost uncontrollable desire to go in the opposite direction. God pointed one way and all my "ideals" pointed in the other. It was when Jonas was traveling as fast as he could away from Nineveh, towards Tharsis, that

he was thrown overboard, and swallowed by a whale which took him where God wanted him to go.[6]

I find myself identifying with Jonah and with Merton in my struggle not just to know the divine will but to do it when it is not what I really want to do. And how God must laugh, the God whom I affirm as omnipresent and omniscient, when I try to sneak away on some vessel of my own choosing. I go below deck to bury myself ostrichlike in the darkness of sleep, so I no longer hear the compelling voice. But God never seems to run short of winds to hurl down upon my ship or of whales to transport me through the depths to where I am supposed to be.

Several years ago in New York City I went to a play called *To Whom It May Concern*. The play, designed to bring to awareness the thoughts passing through people's minds as they attend a celebration of the Holy Eucharist, began with the "Collect for Purity" from the Episcopal *Book of Common Prayer*:

> Almighty God, to you all hearts are open, all desires known, and from you no secrets are hid: Cleanse the thoughts of our hearts by the inspiration of your Holy Spirit, that we may perfectly love you, and worthily magnify your holy Name; through Christ our Lord. Amen.[7]

Seated in a darkened church, the audience was startled when someone stood to interrupt the "celebrant" as he arrived at the phrase *all hearts are open*. "All hearts?" asked the speaker. Ignoring the interruption, the actor continued with "all desires known." Another shouted, "All desires? All desires?" When the "priest" said, "From you no secrets are hid," a chorus of people rose from their seats, murmuring in fearful remembrance of things they thought were known only to themselves: "No secrets? No secrets? No secrets?" Through drama we, the audience, could see the funny side of ourselves. Week after week we hear the words, but suddenly the awareness of the distance between what we hear and how we behave became clear. Our hearts *are* open to God; our desires *are* known by God; and no secrets escape God's scrutiny. Yet we live as though God knows only what we choose to expose. For me, the hilarious image of Adam came to mind. Choosing a way contrary to the known will of God, he first tried to cover himself with fig leaves and then hid in the bushes to avoid discovery. Guilt-ridden and afraid, he peeped between the leaves as he heard the Creator approach saying, "Where are you?" And in my memory I return to kindergarten and a day of making cut-out paper dolls to color. One snip too many, and I ruined mine. To avoid discovery I wadded it up and stuffed it into the inkwell, forgetting that the teacher would expect a product at day's end.

Where are you? God comes again and again with the question, playing the game of hide-and-go-seek we construct, like the parent who knows perfectly well where we are but is patient with our fantasies. Sometimes the game is fun, but often the hiding takes a serious turn. Then we hope that we will find some place small and dark enough to protect us from ever having to own up to the choice we have made. Jonah sleeps soundly in the bowels of the ship while the foreign sailors battle the elements and call upon their gods for aid. Finally someone has the wit to suggest they have a Jonah on board; they awaken the fugitive from his dreams of escape and hold him accountable for the inclement weather. Jonah's moment of reckoning with himself has come. He owns his responsibility and offers himself as victim to satisfy divine wrath. Ironically, he gives himself up for the sake of these foreigners who suffer because of his unwillingness to speak God's judgment and mercy to others outside the covenant community! The attempt to escape God's call to mission often involves little logic.

During my childhood days in England I delighted in Rudyard Kipling's *Just So Stories*, read to me night after night by a mother who knew the magic of storytelling. A favorite was, "How the Whale Got Its Throat," a parody of the book of Jonah, in which a whale swallows a sailor. The sailor, a man "of infinite resource and sagacity," unhooks his suspenders and stretches them across the whale's throat so the creature cannot swallow him! However, in the biblical account, not until he finds himself engulfed by the consequences of his willful ploys does Jonah discover a sagaciousness that moves him to change. In the belly of the fish Jonah reopens the conversation with God. The man who thought a ship could take him beyond the divine presence appears to have no difficulty believing that God will hear him in that dark, slimy place, fathoms down in the ocean! The psalm in Jonah 2:2-10 is a cry for help: "I called to the Lord out of my distress"; a recital of current dis-ease: "You cast me into the deep,...I am driven away from your sight...I went down to the land whose bars closed upon me"; a celebration of deliverance: "You brought up my life from the Pit..."; and contains a promise by the prophet to do what God asks: "What I have vowed I will pay." In response to Jonah's prayer "the Lord spoke to the fish, and it spewed Jonah out upon the dry land."

Perhaps this point in the story generates the greatest mirth. I picture Jonah dazed, stinking of fish, sprawled upon some empty beach and a relieved whale breaching with joy at liberation from a long bout with indigestion! I laugh at Jonah, but in reality I laugh at myself and at the many times I have found myself transported by unorthodox means to a place I did not choose by a God I thought I could outwit. Often the sagacity I need comes through dreams that plunge me into the depths of my unconscious in order to teach the wisdom my rational mind does not willingly grasp. Dreams too are often filled with humor because God knows I learn best when I can smile and relax into an acceptance of the truth I try to deny.

Several years ago I dreamed of being onboard the *Queen Elizabeth 2* (*QE2*) Atlantic liner that was trapped in a lock. Water poured in from behind and had reached such a high level that the turbulence rocked the ship dangerously. I wanted someone to open the gate near the prow of the ship and lower the water level so we could proceed safely, for I feared that before long the water would propel the liner over the top of the lock gate. In my dream the ship did plunge over the top, but then I saw it steam away across a wide expanse of ocean leaving a broad wake behind it. The dream coincided with a time when God was asking me to take a strong, public position that would upset some people and probably result in hostility toward me. I remembered past experience and how I felt when criticized, misunderstood, and shunned for speaking out. Surely I had done my bit for justice making, and it was unreasonable of God to propel me into conflict again. I kept quiet (tried to sleep below deck) until the night I had this whale of a dream.

Pondering the images of the dream, I saw myself as the vessel carrying many "passengers." These included fear of rejection and cultural expectations as well as the desire for peer recognition and the imprimatur of ecclesiastical authority. Nonaction caused me to feel "locked in" to a place where the turbulence of resisting God's call battered me. Finally what I feared most happened: I found myself propelled (spewed) forward to where I needed to be. This dream brought me through the depths of *metanoia* to a place of acquiescence, if not joyful response, to the divine will. I went to Nineveh.

The third chapter of the book opens with God's asking Jonah again to go and preach. This time "Jonah set out and went to

Nineveh, according to the word of the Lord" (Jon. 3:3). His successful preaching led the king of Nineveh and all his subjects to repentance and fasting, and God had mercy on the city. It sounds like a preacher's dream, but the success of his mission did not make Jonah rejoice. Divine intervention had made him assent to God's call, but deep conversion of heart had not taken place. He did not like the Assyrians now any more than he had at the beginning. He still perceived them as the enemy, pagan outsiders. He had hoped his mission would fail. Jonah found himself caught in the dilemma created by God's eagerness to embrace and forgive and his own desire to exclude and to judge. Nineveh painfully challenged Jonah's prejudice. He ended up angry, resentful, and petulant under the hot desert sun.

I believe this story ends where it does in order to confront us with our own struggle to see as God sees and act as God requires. The inclination to close ranks and to discriminate between those who are acceptable and those who do not really belong is ever present. We may utter pious platitudes about those whose economic status, religious tradition, racial background, or sexual orientation differs from our own. But we would prefer not to deal with the challenge to include them fully in our community. Perhaps the greatest gift Jonah offers is to mirror our own imperfections, our mixed motives, our need for continuing conversion of life as we discern God's will and deal with our resistances to it. He brings us down to earth, to *humus*, from the lofty heights of our imagined spiritual maturity to our "mixed-up-ness." Jonah helps us accept our full *humanity*, which is *humility*, by allowing us to laugh, by *humor*. It is surely no accident that these three words—*humanity, humility, humor*—share a common root, for they are inextricably interconnected.

Not until he was alone inside the fish did Jonah, like the

prodigal, come to himself (Luke 15:17). Those moments of self-realization began the homecoming, the journey toward wholeness that lasts a lifetime. Jonah did not become the perfect, obedient, open-minded, faith-filled servant of God we might have hoped for in order to append a "happy ever after" ending to the story. Dire need brought him to obedience, just as hunger and poverty motivated the return of the reckless son. But the dialogue with God was reopened. The God who yearned to forgive Nineveh also had arms open to welcome Jonah home. We also come, again and again, to make our response to a loving Creator, knowing that while far from single-minded we consent to deal with the reality of who we are and the incongruities with which we live.

This is the Benedictine way. This is our way as we consent to change by translating into action the holy teachings of a patient God.

A JOURNAL ENTRY

August 9, 1996

God has no sharp edges! This thought came to me as I sat before my icon of Mary embracing a small but adult looking Christ, an image of loving embrace. My body was there but I found my mind wandering and my hands fidgety, so began harshly to judge my ability to be present. God seemed to invite me to accept the restlessness and come back into conscious prayer each time I became aware of "going away." I am looking forward to a time of retreat next week but this can keep me from being present now and accepting that this day promises to be a busy one. Today I want to find the divine in the midst of the mundane, and that will take a change of attitude. God's love can be tough; God's call can lead me into some painful places, but there are no sharp edges!

HOLY ONE, hold me; envelop me in compassion because I am not yet who you made me to be. When I am tempted to fill up the empty spaces with things that create a deeper emptiness, lead me into the fullness of your grace. Let me walk with you today, and if I stray along byways of my own choosing, turn me around and bring me home. Amen.

SUGGESTIONS FOR REFLECTION

1. Scripture passage for *lectio divina*: Luke 19:1-10.

2. We often use our imagination to give form to Christ as we try to follow him day by day. Try turning that concept around and ask yourself, "How does Christ see me?" Take some time to relax, breathe deeply, become still, and then allow your imagination to suggest a place where you are sitting, walking, standing. Notice what you are wearing, the expression on your face, the way your body feels as you sense Christ looking at you. What does he see? Allow him to speak your name and tell you whatever you need to hear. Allow a dialogue to develop; and when you are ready, record the conversation in your journal. Consider whether you want to make any changes as you continue your pilgrimage.

NINE

OBEDIENCE

*The labor of obedience will bring you back
to him from whom you had drifted through the sloth of
disobedience. This message of mine is for you, then, if you
are ready to give up your own will, once and for all,
and armed with the strong and noble weapons of
obedience to do battle for the true King,
Christt the Lord.*[1]

THE YOUNG DAUGHTER of a friend of mine was exasperated with her mother one day when the final demand that she clean up her room included sanctions if she failed to comply. Procrastination had finally caught up with her. Looking at the distasteful task, the child exploded, "Momma, every time you say must, it makes me go won't all over!" I understand the feeling. There is something very fundamental in human nature that rebels against rules, requirements, and commands that challenge our self-will. Eve looks at the tree she and Adam are forbidden to touch, and it is the only one that attracts. The posted speed limit is 55 miles per hour, so I push up to 64 though there is no urgency about getting to my destination. An employer insists that staff take only an hour for lunch, but by leaving a few minutes early and returning a few minutes late they manage to stretch the time to one hour and fifteen minutes. We do not readily embrace obedience, and we often expend a great deal of energy in attempts to avoid doing what is required of us. Obedience is hard work (Saint Benedict calls it labor), for it demands of us a searching honesty about our willfulness and challenges our claims of independence.

Jesus turns to his listeners on one occasion and asks them, "Why do you call me 'Lord, Lord,' and do not do what I tell you?" (Luke 6:46). He confronts them with the assumption that by giving him a title of honor they earn his respect and belong in his company. No, says Jesus, that involves a labor of obedience, an effort to shovel away the debris of deception in order to build a life of faithful service. A telling little parable that follows reinforces his words:

> I will show you what someone is like who comes to me, hears my words, and acts on them. That one is like a man building a house, who dug deeply and laid the foundation on rock; when a flood arose, the river burst against that house but could not shake it, because it had been well built. But the one who hears and does not act is like a man who built a house on the ground without a foundation. When the river burst against it, immediately it fell, and great was the ruin of that house (Luke 6:47-49).

The Rule of Saint Benedict calls monks again and again to listen—listen to God's word, listen to the abbot, listen to one another because this is the way of Christian formation, the way of obedience. The rule orders community life in such a way that every activity, all time, and each relationship provides an opportunity to hear God's word and act upon it. The kind of listening Benedict calls for is a deep hearing that moves beyond understanding with the mind to a willingness for the heart to be moved. Because ear and heart are inextricably connected, obedience to God's call follows. So Saint Benedict begins the Prologue by saying, "Listen carefully, my [child], to the master's instructions, and attend to them with the ear of your heart. This is advice from a [parent] who loves you; welcome it, and faithfully put it into practice."[2]

A few verses later, Benedict urges the monk to wake up, take action, and respond to the divine word:

> Let us get up then, at long last, for the Scriptures rouse us when they say, *It is high time for us to arise from sleep* (Rom. 13:11). Let us open our eyes to the light that comes from God, and our ears to the voice from heaven that every day calls out this charge: *If you hear his voice today, do not harden your hearts.*[3]

One of the characteristics of the Rule is its personal nature. While Benedict gives detailed instructions for the ordering of community life, he never forgets that he is dealing with individuals who have different needs, temperaments, and experience in the life of prayer. He speaks clearly of the kind of discipline appropriate for each monk and strives for compassion and understanding on the part of those in leadership. The abbot is to be "as Christ"—patient, gentle, respectful of the dignity of his monks, yet always challenging them to stretch and grow as they listen attentively to God. The primary obedience called for is willing response to the personal word of God—but first the word must be heard. The Latin word *obsculta* (listen) has the same root as *oedire,* translated into English as "obedience." The rote mouthing of prayers or doing of duty does not constitute obedience but rather the open-hearted listening to God with a willingness to change.

Obedience through Persistence

Sometimes obedience consists of not giving up when efforts to listen to God through scripture seem unrewarding and when abandoning the attempt and opting for a less demanding activity seems easier. I often feel tempted to give up, but on one occasion my inability to focus and my decision not to give up taught me more than I might have understood at a time when I was able to be more attentive. That morning I sat with Bible, prayer book, candle, and strong coffee, trying to be still in the awareness of God's presence. Beneath me I heard the jarring sound of heavy industrial fans drying out a basement from which six inches of flood water had just been drained. Outside fog blurred the trees, a metaphor for the cloudy muddle through which I tried to pass in my attempt to pray. I could not stay focused on scripture, and inner quietness escaped me. Then I remembered a collect that seemed to describe my experience and give me hope:

> Almighty God, you alone can bring into order the unruly wills and affections of sinners: Grant your people grace to love what you command and desire what you promise; that, among the swift and varied changes of the world, our hearts may surely there be fixed where true joys are to be found; through Jesus Christ our Lord, who lives and reigns with you and the Holy Spirit, one God, now and for ever. Amen.[4]

Unruly thoughts and desires seemed to be the order of the day; they just wouldn't stay in place, no matter how hard I tried to marshal them. That collect described the experience. Hope was embodied in the statement that only God can bring order to the scattered confusion and grace us with the capacity to realign our wills and affections. It takes a letting go on our part, an acknowledgment that we are not in control, to open up the space that allows God to fix our hearts where joy is.

So often our first reaction to muddle is to clear it up, to organize, control, or fix the problems rather than ask what we might learn from the experience. We close our hearts to the distasteful parts of life that challenge us to listen for God's voice, to acknowledge our limitations, and to grow. We lose touch with our deepest heart-life, hardening ourselves against the acknowledgment that God speaks the life-enhancing word that invites change. Hardness of heart is a refusal to listen, an avoidance of obedience.

My awareness of my struggle to pray that morning caused me to stop trying and ask, "What is this all about? Where is God's word to me? What may I learn from the inattentiveness and confusion?" I first realized that tiredness played a major role in my inability to stay focused. An intensely busy three days, overnight guests, and trying to find someone who would come during the weekend to pump out the basement had left me drained of energy. It was both unrealistic and arrogant to think that I could be as energetically attentive as I would like, and God's invitation was to rest, let go, acknowledge the imperfection of my prayer, and offer it for God's redeeming action.

This insight, simple but necessary, caused me to look at my resistance to letting go of the way I wanted things to be. I was invited to accept the less than satisfying prayer time instead of fantasizing some mature, contemplative mode that I "ought" to be achieving. God was calling upon me to change, to allow divine grace to carry me instead of clutching at an idealized concept of prayer.

When prayer moves from head to heart, we begin to experience an intimacy with God that creates discomfort, because we become aware of the ingenious roadblocks we have erected to keep our distance. The awareness of God's numinous presence puts us powerfully in touch with our creatureliness, the willful choices, and egotistical desires that govern our actions; and we are asked to change. At that point we are stopped in our tracks; we may choose between "business as usual" or a radically new way of being, between obedience and hardness of heart. And, like Moses, we may take off our shoes in the presence of the holy but still need to struggle with our resistance to the life-changing response that God desires.

Saint Benedict also acknowledges this universal human dilemma and the constant need to be open to change. As we have seen already, a monk's first vow was stability, which in Benedict's day usually meant a commitment to remain within the cloister until death. However, the vow also embodied the willingness to be a faithful Christian in the place, condition, circumstance, and relationships of the present moment. Benedict recognizes that prayer takes place in the ordinariness of work, among people who may or may not be attractive to us, at times of joy and when circumstances cause distress. Stability means refusing easy escape routes and finding God in the vicissitudes of life regardless of our sense of the divine presence. The second vow addresses the difficult process of change into which we are always being drawn, for stability is not to be identified with stasis. By this vow the monks also consented to the process of *conversion* of life, to *metanoia*, to that turning that always moves us closer to grace. The psalmist's imperative reminded them daily, "If you hear his voice today, do not harden your hearts" (Ps. 95:7-8; see also Heb. 4:7). Each evening provided an opportunity to search the consciousness for moments of hard-heartedness and to respond with repentance.

Into my morning muddle light was thrown, illuminating with a harsh brilliance the opportunity to stay with my lack of control (stability), open myself to dependence on God's grace (conversion), and go on listening for the word beneath the cacophony of disordered desires so that I might act upon it (obedience). I took my shoes off all right; but as the day unfolded, I found myself wanting to escape the challenge to do what I needed to do in order to walk in God's way. I didn't exactly argue with God as Moses did, but soon my self-sufficient, competent mode that denied the needs of my body took over. It took a while to acknowledge that I needed to set aside a writing project and instead try to be with God as I did some kitchen chores, then walk on the waterlogged ground by a lake filled to capacity, and finally sit at home with a good book.

Letting God work in our lives to bring into order our unruly wills and affections means relinquishing our lofty expectations that we can achieve equilibrium in our soul life. We need to allow for seasons of the spirit and to recognize that we are not disembodied beings but people made to serve God with our full humanity. Christ, as the Word, "became flesh and lived among us," affirming our humanness, experiencing the full range of human need and emotion yet remaining open-hearted in his response to God. Though stretched to the breaking point in Gethsemane, he did not harden his heart; he remained *stable* in his commitment and faithfulness in the present, painful moment; he allowed for *conversion* by setting aside his own desire for the success of his mission; and in his yes he expressed unquestioning *obedience* to the One he addressed intimately as *Abba*.

Gethsemane was a truly dark season for Christ. The struggle took place at night, reflecting the experience of not knowing, of waiting, of letting be—a necessary element in the growth process. The Fourth Gospel uses the metaphor of darkness and gestation to stress the importance of waiting for God's time of harvest. In this story we find the universal experience of loss that plunges us into anguish, evokes cries for help in our weakness, and invites trust in God who is in, under, and beyond the present affliction. The alternative to trusting and letting go is disobedience, which refuses the grace available to us in our ordeal.

Love as the Motive for Obedience

In a culture that encourages individualism and control, monasticism shows us a different way. By consenting to the Rule and taking lifelong vows, the monastic chooses what will control him or her. The monastic understands the call to follow Christ as radical obedience that puts God's will first, lets go of personal property and preferences, and accepts the limitations of corporate life. The abbot's word and the community's collective wisdom set the parameters for individual service. A long period of discernment and testing is required to ensure that this commitment is fully understood and freely made. As Jesus faced testing in the wilderness prior to beginning his ministry, so the would-be monk must confront his desire for immediate gratification, human adulation, and the exploitation of gifts for personal aggrandizement. Like Benedict, alone in his cave above Lake Subiaco, he must spend enough time in silence learning who he is and what he really wants before consenting to life in community.

Benedict is clear that the motive for entering the cloister is love—love for God that supersedes all other desires. The monastic life is not escapism but a call to engage the enemies of gospel living, especially the crippling fears that challenge faith.

> It is love that impels them to pursue everlasting life; therefore, they are eager to take the narrow road of which the Lord says: *Narrow is the road that leads to life* (Matt. 7:14). They no longer live by their own judgment, giving in to their whims

and appetites; rather they walk according to another's decisions and directions, choosing to live in monasteries.... This very obedience, however, will be acceptable to God and agreeable to (others) only if compliance with what is commanded is not cringing or sluggish or half-hearted, but free from any grumbling or any reaction of unwillingness.[5]

Obedience in Benedictine spirituality becomes the means that unifies the community and focuses attention on God as the center of corporate and individual life. Jesus said in Gethsemane, "Not my will but yours be done"; love for God, who was testing him to the limits, enabled Jesus to say yes as he trusted himself to the divine purpose.

Where has our obedience to Jesus' call to follow taken us? To whom are we accountable on this journey? In what ways are we being asked to listen to the word and then to *do* what God asks? These questions come to us who read Saint Benedict today and who seek to interpret the Rule in terms of our life outside the cloister. Because answering them will take time, we may need to set aside a day or weekend retreat time to reflect upon them. We may need to consider our attitude toward obedience, for not all obedience is healthy. Do we too readily give unquestioning obedience and power to another? Are we too dependent on the opinions of others, unwilling to support the truth as we understand it? Do we claim responsibility only for ourselves? Are we tempted to dominate decision-making processes rather than listen to others? Above all, are we willing to struggle, wait, and listen for God's voice so we can *do* what we are asked?

Obedience as Waiting

Jesus said, "Unless a grain of wheat falls into the earth and dies, it remains just a single grain; but if it dies, it bears much fruit" (John 12:24). The seasonal pull into darkness and dormancy plunges us into the realm of not knowing, where waiting with helpless trust strengthens the fibers of our soul until it is time to reclaim life. Disobedience inclines us to force our way back up into light prematurely and with disastrous results when the biting winter frost settles on the new shoots. There are things to be learned in darkness that cannot be comprehended elsewhere.

What kind of life does my heart want? I find no easy answers to that question, but I know the answer means giving up the fantasy of always moving forward and allowing instead for seasons of dormancy. And it is always time to listen. Perhaps the heart's single greatest desire is to listen attentively to the voice of God speaking through scripture, nature, daily events, and the kind of reflection that leads to expanding self-knowledge that refuses to idolize a single narcissistic image. My heart wants the kind of life that leaves room for God to break through the crusty, protective surface that, like Holman Hunt's painting of the Christ figure awaiting admittance to his true home, would keep the divine Word outside. It is the kind of life I find when I listen with the ear of my heart.

Benedict gives detailed instructions on the various rotating duties, none based on personal preference. Here we see obedience expressed through work and the mundane requirements of each day. The emphasis on loving service of one another exempts no one. Even sick or weak brothers were given a type of work or craft that would busy them without overwhelming, so they too might know their place within the community. Just as there were no personal possessions allowed within the community, so obedient performance of tasks and instructions reflected the common life embraced at the vow ceremony.

All this emphasis on obedience may seem a far cry from

what most of us experience in terms of our work in the world or even in our faith communities. Individualism and competition deprive us of a sense of belonging, and all too often we no longer see a connection between our work and the end product. Sometimes financial constraints compel us to function in hostile places and to engage in routine work that does not bring any sense of satisfaction.

Competition and power struggles even encumber our churches. Often the gentle humility of the annual footwashing ceremony practiced in many congregations mocks our responses to one another the rest of the year. Obedience in the workplace, and the obedience that is embodied in listening to other believers and embracing opportunities for spiritual formation, challenges us. Because it challenged Benedict's monks too, maybe we can glean from the Rule some guidelines for doing what God asks of us in our very different time and place.

The key to attentive performance of duties lies in the place we give to reflection on scripture—to *lectio divina*—and the choice we make to carry the word with us during the day. Sometimes a short phrase or word can become a mantra we repeat during repetitive tasks that do not demand intense thought. *Maranatha* ("Our Lord, come") represents a readiness to recognize Christ's presence as we wash dishes, mow the lawn, or fold the laundry; we may begin to express thanksgiving for house, family, and adequate material goods.

Maybe our reading has focused on Jesus' challenging injustice, which increases our awareness of discriminatory practices in the workplace. Where does obedience take us? Perhaps we can no longer be observers, holding anger and discomfort within but must find ways to speak the truth to power, regardless of how our reputation or promotion might be affected. Or perhaps I have heard Peter ask Jesus how many times he must forgive a brother, triggering an awareness of my resentment of a colleague who engineered a work assignment I wanted. Obedience requires a letting go of unwillingness to forgive and forging a relationship of honest encounter and listening that makes cooperation possible. Ultimately listening, reflecting, and commitment to a discernment process may lead to radical change. It may involve leaving a position that conflicts with Christian principles and opting for a less well paid job with an ethically sound company.

Sometimes geography or economic considerations severely limit work choices. For Mary, leaving a work environment that had become increasingly oppressive was not an option. She would lose a long service pension, and few teaching locations could use her special skills. Students with severe learning disabilities set forth a daily challenge; funding cutbacks limited resources. Mary felt trapped by a system that did not always seem to have the students' best interests at heart and that increasingly disregarded the teachers' professionalism. How could she interpret Saint Benedict's call for faithful obedience in this daily battle for the attention of her students?

One of the many strategies Mary adopted was to create a huge "smiley face" that she pinned up at the back of her classroom. When she felt exasperated, she would look up and see a reminder to rejoice and inwardly recall the blessings so often forgotten when circumstances seem overwhelming. Then she discovered that instead of scolding a particularly belligerent student, she could look beyond him or her and allow a broad smile to grow on her face. The student would turn to see the cause of her smile, and disruptive behavior changed to laughter! Mary learned that she had power and freedom to shape her work situation instead of feeling shackled by it.

In her book *Friend of the Soul*, Norvene Vest explores a

Benedictine experience of work, dealing creatively with many contemporary struggles that Benedict could never have envisioned. She writes,

> Widespread assumptions about power and freedom prevent us from thinking clearly about the meaning of work and its connection to wholeness of life. We focus instead on our sense of powerlessness or our lack of freedom to create the conditions that would enable us to experience work as a sacred task, and we become stuck in these notions because they feed into the dominant mythology and draw us back into its limitations. But there is a different way to approach our frustrations with work, although at first it may seem strange to us: it is through a valuing of authority and obedience in community, which can open up new ways of embodying freedom in God.[6]

Listening in order to obey God's word is not always easy, and we bring our own predilections, fears, and prior experiences to the process. Often clarity eludes us or resistance grows when we sense that doing what God asks of us demands change. We have no abbot present to instruct and often lack a community that tempers what we want with the needs of those committed to the same lifestyle. These limitations offer us an opportunity to follow the example of Christians down the centuries who have chosen accountability by finding a spiritual guide to offer objective encouragement along the way. The early desert Ammas and Abbas, women and men of faith, withdrew to the wilderness to find silence and to pray. Soon others came seeking guidance, and their pithy sayings and down-to-earth wisdom enabled many to hear God's word in the ordinariness of daily life and work.

Finding someone to journey with us as soul friend, spiritual director or guide, is a first and major step toward choosing obedience over self-will. The person we share our soul life with does not necessarily need to be a clergy person or someone trained in the art of spiritual direction but a faithful listener who evidences love for God. Meeting monthly or at other agreed-upon intervals makes the commitment to grow in faithful obedience a reality and helps us recognize the sidetracks that move us away from God's will. In some cases, forming a group to offer spiritual guidance may help, especially if members avoid the temptation simply to discuss current issues and stay focused on one another's walk with God.

For Saint Benedict obedience represents a choice to take the narrow road; he does not suggest that this way is easy, but he believes that it leads to fullness of life. The narrow way calls upon us to act willingly in response to the voice of authority and to know that our ultimate authority is God, whose word we hear through scripture, experience, and other persons.

A JOURNAL ENTRY

January 3, 1995

What is this the day for? The question comes in terms of the question, "Which of the many things awaiting my attention will I choose?" but the answer suggests itself in the words of Roger Schutz: *This Day Belongs to God*! I am aware of how privileged I am to be presented with such a choice, and I lift up those without work, people in sweatshops and low paying or humiliating jobs, those unable to choose because of mental or physical disability. My cold persists and reminds me of the blessing of good health, and adequate health insurance ...I glance up and see the little turtle that B. gave me. Turtles spend time in the murky depths but surface when they need air. This day for

God, nothing spectacular, but a willingness to be present in the murk or in the above-water air, breathing in grace and doing what the Word requires.

LIVING GOD, you spoke at the beginning of time, and all things came to be. In Jesus, the Word became flesh bringing grace and authority to the fears and confusion of humankind. Help us hear your voice today and run quickly to obey your life-giving commands. We pray through Jesus the Christ. Amen.

SUGGESTIONS FOR REFLECTION

1. Scripture passage for *lectio divina*: Luke 18:18-25.

2. Draw a time line of your life and mark times when you have sensed God's asking you to take a specific action. How did you respond? If there were times when you said no, consider whether God still asks you to act on those issues. Where you, like Mary, said yes to God's will, notice the feelings, consequences, and results of your action. Dialogue with God in your journal about issues of obedience and your life experience.

3. What does God ask you to do or to be at this time? What situations in your home, workplace, or the wider community call for conversion? How might you be an agent of change in these places?

TEN

LIFE AS PILGRIMAGE

❧

Are you hastening toward your heavenly home?
Then with Christ's help, keep this little rule that we
have written for beginners. After that, you can set
out for the loftier summits of the teaching and
virtues we mentioned above, and under God's
protection you will reach them. Amen.[1]

FROM EARLIEST TIMES God's people have set out on pilgrimage, often like Abraham and Sarah, not knowing where they were going. For some a personal crisis gave impetus to the journey. This was true for Jacob, whose flight from a family alienated by his own deception led to a transformative encounter with Yahweh, the God he could not escape by running away. Those who left Egypt under the leadership of Moses found the long, hazardous journey through the wilderness region of the Sinai formative, compelling them to face fear, doubt, and struggle as they moved circuitously toward a land of promise. In the Hebrew-Christian tradition there are countless stories of individuals with a sense of call to journey forth, often into wilderness areas, so that they might hear the voice of God in uncluttered silence. Again and again people of faith have discovered that an inner journey takes place as they embark on an outer pilgrimage, a movement with and toward God and full of the surprises of the Holy Spirit.

Saint Benedict left Rome for his hillside cave above Lake Subiaco, responding to an inner call, a hunger for God that drove him into solitude. Others on a similar journey joined him, and as we have seen, he crafted his Rule to support, guide, and instruct them on their way. Monks are not finished people. The journey to the monastery, the long period of testing, the process of formation leading to the vow ceremony only begin the lifelong pilgrimage. Thus, at the end of the Rule, Benedict asks if the monks still hasten toward God and home as he encourages them to stay on pilgrimage, since the end of the journey lies beyond mortal life.

Remembering: Stories of Encouragement

Marking stages of the journey is an important means of bringing to consciousness our own experience of grace as well as our connection with those who have gone before who still encourage us through their faith stories. In the monastery the liturgical seasons give shape to the year, recalling the major events of salvation history in which we all participate. Monastic houses celebrate anniversaries, honor saints' days, hold feasts and fasts. Traditions associated with a particular monastic house are designed to enable participants to recall the past, embrace the present, and trust the future. These events and activities are not repeated out of a nostalgic longing for what has been; rather, they remind us of where we are, who we are, and what God is inviting us to become as we continue on the way.

Joshua 3 records the story of God's people finally crossing the Jordan into the Promised Land. After many years of wandering, Joshua orchestrates this boundary-passing event at Yahweh's bidding, telling the Israelites that they will know that the living God is among them because "when the soles of the feet of the priests who bear the ark of the Lord, the Lord of all the earth, rest in the waters of the Jordan, the waters of the Jordan flowing from above shall be cut off" (Josh. 3:13). Joshua then selects twelve men, one from each tribe. He tells them to take a stone from the Jordan and carry it on their shoulders to the place where the people will make camp. The stones will be a sign, so that when children of a later generation ask, "What do these stones mean to you?" (Josh. 4:6) they will hear the story of God's presence among the community through struggle and deliverance. The stones will remain as a witness to past grace and as an invitation to participate in the continuing story and the unfolding pilgrimage.

"What do these stones mean to you?" My *lectio divina* with this passage provokes memories of my journey in Christ, a journey that has taken place within the community of faith yet has required times of solitariness for understanding and growth. Stones frequently have marked the way, sometimes intentionally gathered to symbolize thanksgiving in fellowship with others, sometimes present at a point of personal transition. Some stones, already in place, bore witness to the faith of forebears; other stones seemed like silent stumbling blocks until I consented to spend time with them. Often, like Jacob, I have found the hard pillow-stone in the wilderness to be the place of theophany that led to transformation (Gen. 28:10-22).

Grace comes to us in our wayward solitariness to remind us that we come from God and belong together with God, to whom the Hebrew Scriptures frequently refer as a rock. So that

God's people might remember who they are, a holy community extending in time as well as space, the author of Isaiah writes, "Look to the rock from which you were hewn, and to the quarry from which you were dug" (Isa. 51:1). Stones can help us recognize the relationship between our contemporary faith journey in Christ and the history of God's pilgrimage people in past times.

On the wild and windy shore of the small island of Iona off Scotland's western coast there are ancient stone mounds thought to date back many centuries. Tradition suggests that this is the bay where Columba landed after his hazardous journey across the inhospitable Irish Sea. On this isolated island he founded his great center of monasticism and evangelization. Pilgrimages, undertaken often without clear understanding of destination but with deep faith in God, lord of earth, sky, and ocean, characterized Celtic Christianity. These journeys also led to the establishment of communities where worship, education, learning, and evangelization took place among and through those who gathered in Christ's name. The great weathered stone crosses built in Celtic times continue to draw contemporary pilgrims to wonder and worship. Dwarfed by their size, we find our imagination stirred when we remember those in former times who expressed their faith here.

From Saint Columba's Bay I gathered multicolored pebbles to carry back across the Atlantic and to add to the collection of stones that often help me pray. I hold the stones and ponder my pilgrimage, sometimes aware that the willingness to risk the journey meets with resistance because I like to know where I am going. I want to be in control. These stones challenge me to let go of my demand for certainty and to join the rest of God's vulnerable and fallible travelers who, because they are in Christ, can never settle down into comfortable conform-ity as they follow the displaced Lord. Pilgrimage, risk-taking, is central to faith and is a countercultural choice. The stones ask, "Are you on the journey? Will you confront your fear? Can you find yourself in the timeless procession of saints and sinners traveling hopefully in response to the divine call?"

A pilgrim can reach the island of Lindisfarne off the northeast coast of England by causeway only at low tide. The ruins of the great monastic settlement there bear witness to the once-flourishing community. Saint Cuthbert, sent from Iona to establish a center for study and worship on this remote island, loved solitude. Several delightful legends relate his hunger for prayer and sense of connection with all creatures, including the well-known tale of his spending an entire night of contemplation standing in the ocean. When he finally withdrew at dawn, it is said that the sea otters dried him with their fur before he returned to the cloister!

Cuthbert's desire for greater solitude eventually led to his withdrawal to the even smaller island of Inner Farne, where he lived a spartan life given to prayer, except when the demands of the monastery compelled him to return. This desire for withdrawal from centers of population characterized many Celtic Christians and later, Saint Benedict. Like the pilgrimage theme, solitude also figures prominently in the scriptures. At the beginning of his ministry Jesus withdraws to the desert to listen to God and later invites enthusiastic but soon to be exhausted disciples, "Come away to a deserted place all by yourselves and rest a while" (Mark 6:31).

Stones remind me of the need for solitude and withdrawal from the intense busy-ness that all too often clouds perception and masks loss of direction. Cuthbert found a rock cave with only gulls for company. Memory takes me to a huge stone on a quiet beach of the Long Island Sound. During four week-long and intense doctoral study periods, this stone summoned me each day. It demanded my presence and my silence, telling me to quit the heady, intoxicating wine of reason and simply be, without expectation, in its presence. The rock was too smooth and tall to climb, too large to take and "own," too solid to move. The stone, simply there in its glacial splendor, told me to be there too. Sometimes I resented its imperious call since it seemed to give me so little, yet it gave me all I needed—time to stop and be—so that, when the cacophony of words and ideas finally ceased, I could be still enough to know God, the Rock.

We come to know ourselves as unique beings in Christ during solitary times when we leave the company of others in order to listen to the Word who spoke us into being. For this reason, much of the monastic day was given to individual silence and reflection. But always the bell would sound to summon monks back into the work, routine, and corporate worship—also an essential part of their pilgrimage. Who am I? The answer to this question is framed in the context of the Christian community of which I am a pilgrim part and the even broader human search for truth that transcends the boundaries of my particular religious tradition. But I expand the answer when I choose solitary listening time in order to give God space to define, invite, embrace, and question me.

Solitude and Community

This movement between community and solitariness is woven into the fabric of who we are in Christ. We come individually and make our response to the Word, who invites us to become a new creation and to live in divine intimacy. We nurture our life in Christ as the personal conversation continues and as we gradually learn to do less of the talking and begin to listen. But because our faith commitment joins us to other pilgrims on the way, we are challenged to live the new life together. We become part of that continuing community of God's people who exhibit a willingness to listen to one another. We come with many gifts, foibles, desires, and expectations but also with many different images of how to express our life together in Christ. Perhaps this danger had surfaced in Saint Paul's mind when he wrote to the members of the church in Philippi, begging them to live in mutual respect and then quoting the hymn about Christ's self-emptying.

Make my joy complete: be of the same mind, having the same love, being in full accord and of one mind.

Do nothing from selfish ambition or conceit, but in humility regard others as better than yourselves.

Let each of you look not to your own interests, but to the interests of others. Let the same mind be in you that was in Christ Jesus,
who, though he was in the form of God,
did not regard equality with God
as something to be exploited,
but emptied himself,
taking the form of a slave,
being born in human likeness.
And being found in human form,
he humbled himself
and became obedient to the point of death—
even death on a cross.
Therefore God also highly exalted him
and gave him the name
that is above every name,
so that at the name of Jesus
every knee should bend,
in heaven and on earth and under the earth,

and every tongue should confess
that Jesus Christ is Lord,
to the glory of God the Father (Phil. 2:2-11).

Maybe this danger also explains Saint Benedict's insistence that the community eliminate grumbling and self-interest. As a small child I collected several egg-shaped stones and, with a playmate, made little nests of leaves, believing that the "eggs" would one day hatch! I remember the sharp disappointment when my childish fantasy did not become reality. Yet how often have I harbored the same immature expectation—that persons will become what I want them to be in "my" perfect community?

My years of living with a Benedictine monastic community quickly taught me that the struggles played out in the congregations I had known were present there too. A common desire to live monastic life did not obscure different personalities; our living together constantly called for mutual respect and understanding. How we sang the office, related to guests, spent free time, used monastery resources, and a million other decisions claimed attention and invited willingness to listen to one another. Scripture and the Rule of Saint Benedict were our guides, and I came to value the profound wisdom and down-to-earth guidelines Benedict offers for community. Benedict reminded us that where persons integrate community and solitariness, work and leisure, study and prayer, a more balanced life becomes possible.

Saint Benedict writes his "little rule for beginners" to encourage them to set out on the pilgrim way with Christ as guide, suggesting that only after faithful, daily attention to the details of living together could they begin to ascend the more lofty heights of Christian perfection! I need to hear this too. I am impatient, sometimes running ahead of myself—and God— in the attempt to reach the end without delay. I need to hear the advice of Brother Lawrence, who told an enthusiastic young

sister not to try to "run faster than grace"! I need the word of
Saint Benedict:

> Do not aspire to be called holy before you really are, but first
> be holy that you may truly be called so. Live by God's com-
> mandments every day; treasure chastity, harbor neither hatred
> nor jealousy of anyone, and do nothing out of envy. Do not
> love quarreling; shun arrogance.... And finally, never lose hope
> in God's mercy.[2]

To be on pilgrimage means to be always in formation, always
open to the prompting of the Spirit and the gifts that come
through paying attention to our brothers and sisters.

When the authors of the four Gospels wrote their accounts,
they did not so much create historical records as share a faith
journey. They knew the Jesus of history who lived, taught,
healed, and died somewhere around 30 C.E., not only through
the oral stories handed down but through their own life-changing experience of the Holy Spirit's power as promised by Christ.
These writers were on pilgrimage, living out their faith in diverse
communities that shaped the narratives they recorded. Without
the creeds and confessions of faith that are part of our heritage
and without clear road maps, the Gospel writers needed to
trust their experience and the Hebrew Scriptures that were
foundational to Jesus and themselves. The monotheism with
which they were familiar now had to be broadened to embrace
the reality of Jesus as "the Word made flesh," Son of God, and
the Spirit alive and working in their midst. Years before a clear
definition of the Trinity emerged, they lived with questions
and lack of clarity, wondering even as they found themselves
joyfully compelled to proclaim the good news.

God invites each of us to become like these Gospel authors
as we travel by faith, learning to tell our own good news about

Christ. We are to be fifth Gospel writers! Reflecting on how and when we have been aware of encountering God in the midst of daily life and taking time to know where we are at this moment make our pilgrimage intentional. Keeping a daily journal will prove invaluable as a means of paying attention to the contours of the journey, its pitfalls and moments of victory, the times of waiting and the forward movement that becomes clear through silence. We also come to know more intimately the Christ who, like the good shepherd, goes ahead of us, urging us on, teaching us to trust. And we become more sensitized to the urging of the Spirit, learning to act boldly and expectantly as we step out into the unknown. Above all we learn that there is no place, no mundane activity, no encounter that is divorced from the sacred, for God is ever present, ever loving, and waiting to dance through each day with us.

> Hour by hour keep careful watch over all you do, aware that God's gaze is upon you, wherever you may be. As soon as wrongful thoughts come into your heart, dash them against Christ.[3]

Saint Benedict urges us to live consciously and without fear, even when we find ourselves beset by negative thoughts provoked by anger, envy, resentment, and other "wrongful" attitudes. These are to be cast down at the feet of Christ, relinquished to the One whose life bore witness to the power of forgiveness and whose Spirit empowers us to let go. The image of casting down and relinquishing is not unlike that offered in the timeless human story told in John Bunyan's *The Pilgrim's Progress*. The pilgrim sets out with a burden, and only when he comes to the cross does he find freedom as his heavy load rolls away.

Life in a monastery may seem to those living "in the world"

to be one long retreat or prayer meeting, which is far from the truth, as the Rule makes plain. There is work to be done, guests to be welcomed, missions to be undertaken. The monks' myriad daily tasks of maintaining buildings and grounds consumes a great deal of time. For this reason Benedict ensures uninterrupted times of community retreat for the purpose of prayerful reflection. Today the retreat tradition continues, usually for a period of one to two weeks when guests are not received and no unnecessary work is done. Sometimes a retreat leader will offer meditations to guide members of the community in their discernment of God's call to them at this moment in their journey. Often the time will be left unstructured, giving all the opportunity to sense where they are being led by the Spirit. Throughout the retreat, the monks maintain silence to facilitate the kind of heart listening that Benedict calls for at the beginning of his Rule.

A one- or two-week period of silence in community may sound daunting, but I remember with much gratitude the five long retreats in which I participated. The uncluttered silent time moved me into a different rhythm, which in itself made me conscious of habitual ways of being that prevented awareness. This change in rhythm applied even to prayer times, when I sometimes uncomfortably realized that the familiar had become like a drug that dulled my attentiveness to God. As I became more still, more intentional about listening prayer, I began to hear questions: Where are you? What do you really want? Are you moving forward on the pilgrim way? Are you stuck or choosing sidetracks? Do you know how much I love you and want to walk with you? Have you been hearing the good news that I have been bringing you each day? Once again my journal became an important tool as I asked for the grace to respond honestly and for the willingness to step out in new directions. The retreat was a hard and richly blessed time of learning to know God more intimately.

Today no one tells me that it is time for retreat, so I need to choose that option. There never seems to be time for it, and I know that unless I sit down with my calendar at the beginning of the year, it just won't happen. I try to take a week's retreat once a year and to include a day of silent retreat once a month. Sometimes I spend the longer retreat in a monastic house where the offering of regular chanted worship structures each day and where a member of the community provides some personal guidance.

One such retreat took place in the intense heat of an Alabama summer, where early morning and late evening walks gave me a sense of meeting with the Creator "in the cool of the day." On another occasion I drove deep into the mountains surrounding the Sonoma Valley in California and hiked, accompanied by red-tailed hawks and a faithful lab who adopted me. On this occasion I had no retreat director but sensed God inviting me to let go of my routines, even my saying of the morning "office," and to be open to the book of nature as Saint Anthony was in his mountain retreat many centuries ago. I learned much about my demand for control, my dependence on familiar patterns, and my fear of a totally open time and place in which to listen to the Word.

At times I have chosen a retreat in the Ignatian tradition, when for eight days—and on one occasion thirty days—I have met with a director who helped me enter a discernment process using the *Spiritual Exercises* of Saint Ignatius. I have found these retreats of special importance at transition points in my journey, at those times when I have needed the objective guidance of another who will "hold my feet to the fire" when I would prefer to settle for mediocrity.

Monthly retreat days also have become a necessary spiritual discipline to keep me on track. A nearby retreat house has a small cabin I sometimes use, arriving the night before so that I can stay overnight and wake fresh to begin the day of retreat. On one occasion I checked into an inn on the Blue Ridge Parkway where beautiful views and the absence of telephone and TV offered a quiet space to be. I anticipated wakening to a magnificent panorama of mountains but instead found the whole area sucked into thick fog! Disappointment and frustration filled me until I seemed to hear God inviting me to let go of expectations and to be available to the present moment, allowing it to teach me. Gradually I began to sense an enveloping love, to feel that I was in a cocoon, a place of dormancy and waiting. There was nothing for me to do; I was simply asked to be, allowing God to do what God needed to do in order to bring forth something new. This experience reminded me of Julian of Norwich, who spoke of God's love as a great cloak wrapped around us and of Jesus as our tender mother, whose patience is never exhausted.

Last week I saw the words *Retreat Day* in my calendar and thought ... *impossible! Christmas is ten days away; I am winding down a job that I have held for more than five years; and I have this book to finish with a deadline of December 31.* Half-heartedly I called a couple who offer their home as a place of retreat and asked if I could spend the day there, only to learn that construction and painting made it unavailable. My inclination was to forget the date this time, but an inner voice seemed to tell me that I must honor the commitment. Reluctantly I decided to stay home. I turned off the telephone and let go of all the unfinished tasks in order to make a space for listening. The joy of not activating the alarm clock and then returning to bed with a hot cup of tea after I woke set the tone for the day. Instead of resistance I found joyful anticipation growing. The scripture I read seemed to come alive as never before, and I carried it with me as I walked around the lake and laughed at up-ended ducks scrabbling for the corn I threw them. Later, remembering Saint Benedict's commendation of manual labor, I raked the last of the fallen leaves into neat piles, offering the physical movements of my body as prayer. A thirty-minute silent period before an icon, reading by the log fire I built and preparing some tasty food gave me the sense that I had spent the day unwrapping a precious gift, which I would carry with me into the busy-ness ahead.

Our pilgrimage journey is profoundly blessed when we create nontraveling times in order to see more clearly where we are going. Not everyone can take a week away from family and work responsibilities, but a weekend once a year is often possible. People new to the retreat experience may benefit from guidance. As a first step, consider choosing an organized retreat where a person speaks and offers individual consultation. Most monasteries and convents have guest accommodations, and trained monastics will meet with individuals. Check ahead of time if opting for this kind of retreat.

Apart from the annual retreat, a monthly time for coming apart with God will greatly enhance the journey. Again, giving a full day may be impossible; but a morning, evening, or afternoon offers a good alternative. A retreat may mean planning ahead for childcare, reserving some vacation time, or letting go of a routine activity once a month. Finding a friend willing to make the same commitment may help, especially if, together, you can be silent, only sharing the experience afterward.

Happy are the people whose strength is in you!
   whose hearts are set on the pilgrims' way .
—Psalm 84:4, BCP

The psalmist writes of the blessedness of those journeying not only to the holy city but toward the goal of a deeper knowledge of God. Benedict asks us if we are hastening on this road; a contemporary Benedictine Macrina Wiederkehr calls on us to notice if we have become tourists rather than pilgrims. In a reflection subtitled, "By Their Cameras You Shall Know Them,"[4] she speaks of our tendency to rush from one site to another taking pictures and accumulating souvenirs. As pilgrims we learn to take our time, to lighten our baggage, and to listen for the voice of God that speaks not only in scripture but also through nature, our sisters and brothers, and the mundaneness of daily life. When our hearts are set on the pilgrim way, we step joyfully forward seeing the holy in the ordinary and the whole earth filled with the glory of God. This is the way of Saint Benedict, the path that leads to fullness of life as we travel with our loving Creator.

A JOURNAL ENTRY

September 1, 1988, Holy Savior Priory

Through the screen on the upper portion of my door I just observed a daily miracle—dawn breaking beyond the trees. Irrevocably, slowly, since the beginning of time night has relinquished her hold over the earth, allowing light to energize the world. And nightly the sun gives up its reign. So that sleep, replenishment, and renewal may be received. A small bird comes to sit on the wire outside, twittering a greeting. I know about the changes of days and seasons, but this morning I *see* a little.

God, you create rhythm and make harmony to grace our lives. There is power but no coercion in your omnipotence, gentleness but no sloth in your compassion. You are action and stillness, giver and receiver, dawn and nightfall. The sleeping cows know your times, and the heavy locust jumps to express the life-force you bestow. A breeze moves the tree-tops as raucous crows call out that day is here. And what am I that you are mindful of me, a child of earth that you care for me? The dance has begun again. I join you in the cele-bration of all that is, moving sometimes with ecstasy and abandon, often with hesitant steps in the cosmic harmony. With waltz and tango your glory, shekinah-like, transmutes our life.

I wait this day, O God, to dance, play, work with you. You are all, in all, through all. Reveal your reality by wak-ing me from anesthesia—the dullness that closes me in with my own fearful preoccupations. The glimpse makes me yearn for more perfect sight and for the perceptive vision that is your gift. People like trees walking will do for a start but don't leave me there. Touch me again and again, sur-prising me into seeing, hoping, believing.

GOD OF THE PILGRIM WAY, keep us alert as we travel with you so that we may see the beauty with which you surround us. Help us to identify the unnecessary baggage we carry and with full hearts to step lightly through your world. Amen.

SUGGESTIONS FOR REFLECTION

1. Scripture passage for *lectio divina*: 1 Kings 19:4-12.

2. Using Psalm 84 as a model, write your own psalm expressing desire for God and willingness to keep on the pilgrim way.

3. Create a collage using photos, letters, and other memorabilia to illustrate your life journey with God. You do not need to be an artist! You may include words that describe experiences at major turning points and times of encounter with God. You might want to draw—stick figures will do—or use pictures from magazines. Begin the venture with prayer and allow imagination to lead you. When you have finished, write a one-sentence summary of where you want to go from here.

EXAMEN OF CONSCIOUSNESS

This exercise adapts the Ignatian form of daily self-examination. Approach this exercise with joyful expectation that God will reveal blessings and new directions rather than choosing a negative approach of searching only for what is amiss in your life.

Thanksgiving

Look back over the day and notice where you need to express thankfulness. Do not simply choose what you think you "ought" to be thankful for, but by merely reflecting on the day see what emerges. Notice how you feel toward what is showed to you. Do you see a giftedness in your life? Do you sense your own need? Allow gratitude to take hold of you, and express it to God. Sometimes gratitude will begin with small incidents, especially on difficult days. Notice how your sense of the day changes as you express your thanksgiving.

Asking for Insight

Next pray for guidance, asking the Holy Spirit to show you what you need to see. Do not simply review your own analysis of the day but open your heart to God with the willingness to see what God wants to reveal.

Looking for God

Again look back over the events of the day; this time be aware of when you experienced God's presence in your life. It may be that you were conscious of God in yourself or in others. Notice your interior moods, feelings, urges, movements.

Was there any joy, pain, turmoil, increase of love, anger, harmony, conscious prayer, isolation, or fulfillment present? In what general direction do you feel you are being drawn by God?

How have you been responding to these experiences or situations?

Expressing Repentance and Gratitude

Seek forgiveness from God for the moments when you were unresponsive to the divine presence and love. Pray for a willingness to change those things and attitudes that distance you from the Creator God who loves you. Praise God for those times when you have sensed your closeness and cooperation with God's purpose. Someone has written, "Life takes a lot of consecrating, but when it is lived thankfully, it is well on the way to becoming a holy thing." Reflect on the "holiness" of your life.

Receiving Help and Guidance for Tomorrow

Finally, ask God for what you will need tomorrow. It may be that you want to pray to overcome something or to accept a "thorn in the flesh." Perhaps there is a need for perseverance or for a greater sensitivity to God's presence in your life. Maybe also there are some resentments or attitudes to let go of or a sense that you need to love more. Remember that alone it is difficult to change old patterns, but the Holy Spirit is our strength and support as we try to grow more fully into God's image. You may choose to write your reflections, especially to note the prayer you have made for what you need tomorrow. Expect to be surprised by God's response!

NOTES

All citings from the Rule of Saint Benedict (RB) are taken from *The Rule of Saint Benedict in English*, edited by Timothy Fry, OSB, and published by The Liturgical Press, Collegeville, Minn., 1981.

Introduction
1. RB Prologue 46.
2. RB 32:4.
3. RB 4:20–24.
4. RB Prologue 2.

CHAPTER 1 *Praying the Scriptures*
1. RB 4:55.
2. RB Prologue 49.

CHAPTER 2 *Hospitality*
1. RB 4:20–26.
2. RB 32:1, 4.
3. RB 1:10-11.
4. Jean Pierre de Caussade coined the phrase "the sacrament of the present moment" in his book *Self Abandonment to Divine Providence*, now republished under the title *The Sacrament of the Present Moment* (San Francisco: HarperSanFrancisco, 1989).
5. Dietrich Bonhoeffer, *Life Together* (New York:Harper and Row, 1954), 26.
6. RB 53:1–3, 6–7, 15.
7. RB 66:3–4.
8. Esther de Waal, *Seeking God: The Way of Saint Benedict* (Collegeville, Minn.: The Liturgical Press, 1984), 120–21.
9. RB 53:15.

CHAPTER 3 *Simplicity*

1. RB Prologue 49.
2. Hildegard of Bingen with commentary by Matthew Fox, *Illuminations of Hildegard of Bingen* (Santa Fe, N. Mex.: Bear and Co., 1985), 24.
3. Henry David Thoreau, *Walden*.
4. Gerard Manley Hopkins, "God's Grandeur" from *The New Oxford Book of English Verse 1250–1950* (New York: Oxford University Press, 1972), 786.

CHAPTER 4 *Prayer*

1. RB 52.
2. RB 4:55.
3. RB 19:7.
4. Maxwell Corydon Wheat Jr., *Limulus* (Freeport, N.Y.: Virginia Wheat, 1988), 6.

CHAPTER 5 *Manual Labor*

1. RB 48:1.
2. RB 48:7–8.
3. RB 32:4.
4. Norvene Vest, *Friend of the Soul: A Benedictine Spirituality of Work* (Cambridge, Mass.: Cowley Publications, 1997), 73.

CHAPTER 6 *Rest*

1. RB 48:5.

CHAPTER 7 *Stability*

1. RB 58:1, 9–10.
2. RB Prologue 35.
3. John A. Sanford, *Dreams: God's Forgotten Language* (SanFrancisco: HarperSanFrancisco, 1968, 1989).

CHAPTER 8 *Conversion of Life*

1. RB Prologue 35–37.
2. *Book of Common Prayer*, 265.
3. RB Prologue 2–3.

4. *Returning: Exercises in Repentance*, edited by Jonathan Magonet (London: Reformed Synagogues of Great Britain, 1975), 86.

5. See Appendix for an example of Examen of Consciousness

6. Thomas Merton, *The Sign of Jonas* (New York: Harcourt, Brace & Co., 1953), 10–11.

7. *Book of Common Prayer*, 355.

CHAPTER 9 *Obedience*

1. RB Prologue 2–3.

2. RB Prologue 1.

3. RB Prologue 8–10.

4. *Book of Common Prayer*, 219.

5. RB 5:10–12, 14.

6. Vest, 107.

CHAPTER 10 *Life as Pilgrimage*

1. RB 73:8–9.

2. RB 4:62–69, 74.

3. RB 4:48–50.

4. Macrina Wiederkehr, *Seasons of Your Heart* (San Francisco: Harper-SanFrancisco, 1985), 183.